NorthStar 2
LISTENING & SPEAKING

FOURTH EDITION

Authors	LAURIE FRAZIER
	ROBIN MILLS
Series Editors	FRANCES BOYD
	CAROL NUMRICH

NorthStar: Listening & Speaking Level 2, Fourth Edition

Pearson Education, 10 Bank Street, White Plains, NY 10606

Contributor credit: Lynn Bonesteel

Staff credits: The people who made up the *NorthStar: Listening & Speaking Level 2, Fourth Edition* team, representing editorial, production, design, and manufacturing, are Kimberly Casey, Tracey Cataldo, Rosa Chapinal, Daniel Comstock, Aerin Csigay, Mindy DePalma, Dave Dickey, Graham Fisher, Nancy Flaggman, Niki Lee, Françoise Leffler, Amy McCormick, Mary Perrotta Rich, Robert Ruvo, Christopher Siley, Debbie Sistino, and Ken Volcjak.

Text composition: ElectraGraphics, Inc.
Editorial: Scribble Creative, LLC

Library of Congress Cataloging-in-Publication Data

Frazier, Laurie.
  Northstar 2 : Listening and speaking / Authors : Laurie Frazier, Robin Mills. — Fourth Edition. / Frazier, Laurie.
       pages cm
  ISBN-13: 978-0-13-338213-6 (Level 2) – ISBN 978-0-13-294040-5 (Level 3) – ISBN 978-0-13-338207-5 (Level 4) – ISBN 978-0-13-338214-3 (Level 5)
1. English language—Textbooks for foreign speakers. 2. English language—Spoken English—Problems, exercises, etc. 3. Listening—Problems, exercises, etc. I. Mills, Robin, 1962– II. Title. III. Title: Northstar two. IV. Title: Listening and speaking.
  PE1128.M586 2015
  428.2'4—dc23
                                                                                                    2013050585

Printed in the United States of America

ISBN 10: 0-13-338213-3
ISBN 13: 978-0-13-338213-6

3   17

ISBN 10: 0-13-404979-9 (International Edition)
ISBN 13: 978-0-13-404979-3 (International Edition)

3   17

WELCOME TO
NORTHSTAR

A BLENDED-LEARNING COURSE FOR THE 21ST CENTURY

Building on the success of previous editions, *NorthStar* continues to engage and motivate students through new and updated contemporary, authentic topics in a seamless integration of print and online content. Students will achieve their academic as well as language and personal goals in order to meet the challenges of the 21st century.

New for the FOURTH EDITION

★ Fully Blended MyEnglishLab

NorthStar aims to prepare students for academic success and digital literacy with its fully blended online lab. The innovative new MyEnglishLab: *NorthStar* gives learners immediate feedback— anytime, anywhere—as they complete auto-graded language activities online.

★ NEW and UPDATED THEMES

Current and thought-provoking topics presented in a variety of genres promote intellectual stimulation. The authentic content engages students, links them to language use outside of the classroom, and encourages personal expression and critical thinking.

★ EXPLICIT SKILL INSTRUCTION and PRACTICE

Language skills are highlighted in each unit, providing students with systematic and multiple exposures to language forms and structures in a variety of contexts. Concise presentations and targeted practice in print and online prepare students for academic success.

★ LEARNING OUTCOMES and ASSESSMENT

A variety of assessment tools, including online diagnostic, formative, and summative assessments, and a flexible gradebook, aligned with clearly identified unit learning outcomes, allow teachers to individualize instruction and track student progress.

THE NORTHSTAR APPROACH TO CRITICAL THINKING

What is critical thinking?

Most textbooks include interesting questions for students to discuss and tasks for students to engage in to develop language skills. Often these questions and tasks are labeled critical thinking. Look at this question as an example:

When you buy fruits and vegetables, do you usually look for the cheapest price? Explain.

CONTENTS

The question may inspire a lively discussion with students exploring a variety of viewpoints—but it doesn't necessarily develop critical thinking. Now look at another example:

When people in your neighborhood buy fruits and vegetables, what factors are the most important: the price, the freshness, locally grown, organic (without chemicals)? Make a prediction and explain. How can you find out if your prediction is correct? This question does develop critical thinking. It asks students to make predictions, formulate a hypothesis, and draw a conclusion—all higher-level critical thinking skills. Critical thinking, as philosophers and psychologists suggest, is a sharpening and a broadening of the mind. A critical thinker engages in true problem solving, connects information in novel ways, and challenges assumptions. A critical thinker is a skillful, responsible thinker who is open-minded and has the ability to evaluate information based on evidence. Ultimately, through this process of critical thinking, students are better able to decide what to think, what to say, or what to do.

How do we teach critical thinking?

It is not enough to teach "about" critical thinking. Teaching the theory of critical thinking will not produce critical thinkers. Additionally, it is not enough to simply expose students to good examples of critical thinking without explanation or explicit practice and hope our students will learn by imitation.

Students need to engage in specially designed exercises that aim to improve critical-thinking skills. This approach practices skills both implicitly and explicitly and is embedded in thought-provoking content. Some strategies include:

- subject matter that is carefully selected and exploited so that students learn new concepts and encounter new perspectives.
- students identifying their own assumptions about the world and later challenging them.
- activities that are designed in a way that students answer questions and complete language-learning tasks that may not have black-and-white answers. (Finding THE answer is often less valuable than the process by which answers are derived.)
- activities that engage students in logical thinking, where they support their reasoning and resolve differences with their peers.

Infused throughout each unit of each book, *NorthStar* uses the principles and strategies outlined above, including:

- Make Inferences: inference comprehension questions in every unit
- Vocabulary and Comprehension: categorization activities
- Vocabulary and Synthesize: relationship analyses (analogies); comparisons (Venn diagrams)
- Synthesize: synthesis of information from two texts teaches a "multiplicity" approach rather than a "duality" approach to learning; ideas that seem to be in opposition on the surface may actually intersect and reinforce each other
- Focus on the Topic and Preview: identifying assumptions, recognizing attitudes and values, and then re-evaluating them
- Focus on Writing/Speaking: reasoning and argumentation
- Unit Project: judgment; choosing factual, unbiased information for research projects
- Focus on Writing/Speaking and Express Opinions: decision-making; proposing solutions

THE NORTHSTAR UNIT

1 FOCUS ON THE TOPIC

* **CT** Each unit begins with a photo that draws students into the topic. Focus questions motivate students and encourage them to make personal connections. Students make inferences about and predict the content of the unit.

MyEnglishLab

CT A short self-assessment based on each unit's learning outcomes helps students check what they know and allows teachers to target instruction.

*indicates Critical Thinking

2 FOCUS ON LISTENING

Two contrasting, thought-provoking listening selections from a variety of authentic genres stimulate students intellectually.

CT Students predict content, verify their predictions, and follow up with a variety of tasks that ensure comprehension.

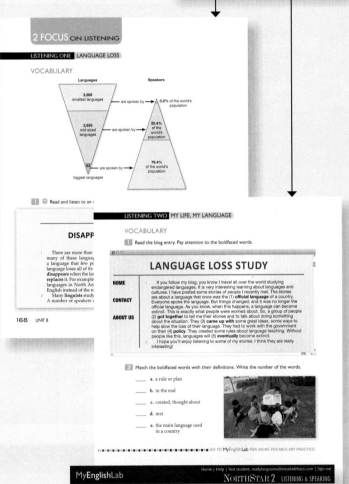

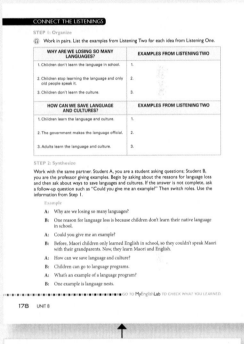

CT Students are challenged to take what they have learned and organize, integrate, and synthesize the information in a meaningful way.

MyEnglishLab

Auto-graded vocabulary practice activities reinforce meaning and pronunciation.

EXPLICIT SKILL INSTRUCTION AND PRACTICE

CT Step-by-step instructions and practice guide students to exercise critical thinking and to dig deeper by asking questions that move beyond the literal meaning of the text.

MAKE INFERENCES

SPEAKER'S VIEWPOINT

An inference is a guess about something that is not directly stated. To make an inference, use information that you understand from what you hear.

A speaker's viewpoint is the speaker's opinion on a subject. Knowing a speaker's viewpoint will help you understand the points made. The speaker's viewpoint is not always stated clearly. You may need to guess or infer the viewpoint.

🎧 Listen to the example. Then read the statement. What is the speaker's viewpoint?

Example

PROFESSOR: Good morning, everybody. Today, I'd like to talk about endangered and dead languages. So . . . who did the reading for today? Hmm . . . I see . . . some of you did . . . Then, who can tell me what a dead language is?

The professor says, "I see some of you did." The professor wants all the students to do the reading and be prepared to discuss. You can infer that he probably would agree that many students are not prepared for class.

🎧 Listen to two excerpts from the lecture. After listening to each excerpt, answer the questions. Discuss your answers with the class.

Excerpt One

Do you think the professor would agree or disagree with the statement: "Language programs are a good way to preserve languages."

    a. agree   **b.** disagree

Excerpt Two

Do you think the student would agree or disagree with the following statement: "I'm not sure it's worth it to preserve languages."?

    a. agree   **b.** disagree

UNIT 8

LISTENING SKILL

LISTENING FOR REASONS AND EXAMPLES

Identifying reasons and examples that support the main idea can help you understand the main idea. Some words and phrases that identify reasons are: *the reason . . . , this is because . . . ,* and *that's why . . .* Some words and phrases that identify and list examples are: *for example . . . , an example of this is . . . , also . . . , for instance . . . ,* and *another . . .*

🎧 Listen to the examples:

Example 1

In school, I learned and spoke English. This is because English was the official language. Everything was taught in English in school. That was the government policy.

  Main idea   In school, I learned and spoke English.

  Reason   This is because English was the official language.

  Reason   That was the government policy.

The main idea is that English was the only language she learned and used in school. The reason is English was the official language and it was the government policy. She says, "This is because English was the official language."

Example 2

Through the language nests, children learn about the values and traditions of the Maori culture. For example, we have a strong belief in love, compassion, caring, hospitality, family responsibilities, and respect for elders. Also, children learn our Maori stories, which are a big part of our tradition.

  Main idea   Through the language nests, children learn about Maori traditions and the basic values of the Maori culture.

  Example   For example, we have a strong belief in love, compassion, caring, hospitality, family responsibilities, and respect for elders.

  Example   Also, children learn our Maori stories, which are a big part of our tradition.

The main idea is the children learn the values and traditions of Maori culture. Examples of values are a strong belief in love, compassion, caring, hospitality, family responsibilities and respect for elders. Another example is children learn about Maori stories, which are part of their tradition.

Explicit skill presentation and practice lead to student mastery and success in an academic environment.

MyEnglishLab

Key listening skills are reinforced and practiced in new contexts. Meaningful and instant feedback provides students and teachers with essential information to monitor progress.

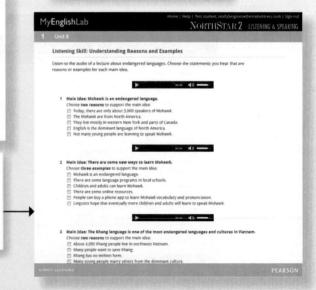

Using models from the unit listening selections, the pronunciation and speaking skill sections expose students to the sounds and patterns of English as well as to functional language that prepares them to express ideas on a higher level.

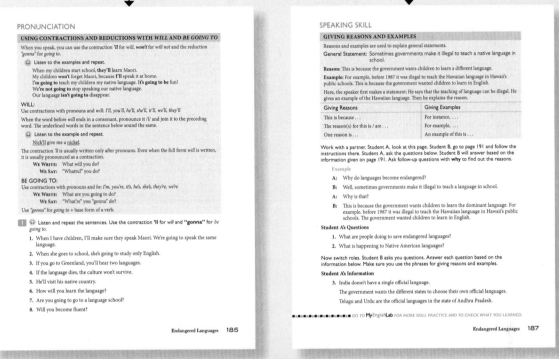

PRONUNCIATION

USING CONTRACTIONS AND REDUCTIONS WITH *WILL* AND *BE GOING TO*

When you speak, you can use the contraction *'ll* for *will*, **won't** for *will not* and the reduction *"gonna"* for *going to*.

Listen to the examples and repeat.

When my children start school, **they'll** learn Maori.
My children **won't** forget Maori, because **I'll** speak it at home.
I'm going to teach my children my native language. **It's going to** be fun!
We**'re not going to** stop speaking our native language.
Our language **isn't going to** disappear.

WILL:
Use contractions with pronouns and *will*: I'll, you'll, he'll, she'll, it'll, we'll, they'll

When the word before *will* ends in a consonant, pronounce it /l/ and join it to the preceding word. The underlined words in the sentence below sound the same.

Listen to the example and repeat.

<u>Nick'll</u> give me a <u>nickel</u>.

The contraction *'ll* is usually written only after pronouns. Even when the full form *will* is written, it is usually pronounced as a contraction.

WE WRITE: What will you do?
WE SAY: "Whattul" you do?

BE GOING TO:
Use contractions with pronouns and *be*: I'm, you're, it's, he's, she's, they're, we're

WE WRITE: What are you going to do?
WE SAY: "What're" you "gonna" do?

Use *"gonna"* for *going to* + base form of a verb.

1. Listen and repeat the sentences. Use the contraction **'ll** for *will* and **"gonna"** for *be going to*.

1. When I have children, I'll make sure they speak Maori. We're going to speak the same language.
2. When she goes to school, she's going to study only English.
3. If you go to Greenland, you'll have two languages.
4. If the language dies, the culture won't survive.
5. He'll visit his native country.
6. How will you learn the language?
7. Are you going to go to a language school?
8. Will you become fluent?

Endangered Languages 185

SPEAKING SKILL

GIVING REASONS AND EXAMPLES

Reasons and examples are used to explain general statements.

General Statement: Sometimes governments make it illegal to teach a native language in school.

Reason: This is because the government wants children to learn a different language.

Example: For example, before 1987 it was illegal to teach the Hawaiian language in Hawaii's public schools. This is because the government wanted children to learn in English.

Here, the speaker first makes a statement: He says that the teaching of language can be illegal. He gives an example of the Hawaiian language. Then he explains the reason.

Giving Reasons	Giving Examples
This is because . . .	For instance, . . .
The reason(s) for this is / are . . .	For example, . . .
One reason is . . .	An example of this is . . .

Work with a partner. Student A, look at this page. Student B, go to page 191 and follow the instructions there. Student A, ask the questions below. Student B will answer based on the information given on page 191. Ask follow-up questions with **why** to find out the reasons.

Example

A: Why do languages become endangered?
B: Well, sometimes governments make it illegal to teach a language in school.
A: Why is that?
B: This is because the government wants children to learn the dominant language. For example, before 1987 it was illegal to teach the Hawaiian language in Hawaii's public schools. The government wanted children to learn in English.

Student A's Questions

1. What are people doing to save endangered languages?
2. What is happening to Native American languages?

Now switch roles. Student B asks you questions. Answer each question based on the information below. Make sure you use the phrases for giving reasons and examples.

Student A's Information

3. India doesn't have a single official language.

The government wants the different states to choose their own official languages.

Telugu and Urdu are the official languages in the state of Andhra Pradesh.

GO TO MyEnglishLab FOR MORE SKILL PRACTICE AND TO CHECK WHAT YOU LEARNED.

Endangered Languages 187

MyEnglishLab

Students continue online practice of key pronunciation and speaking skills with immediate feedback and scoring.

Productive vocabulary targeted in the unit is reviewed, expanded upon, and used creatively in this section and in the final speaking task. Grammar structures useful for the final speaking task are presented and practiced. A concise grammar skills box serves as an excellent reference.

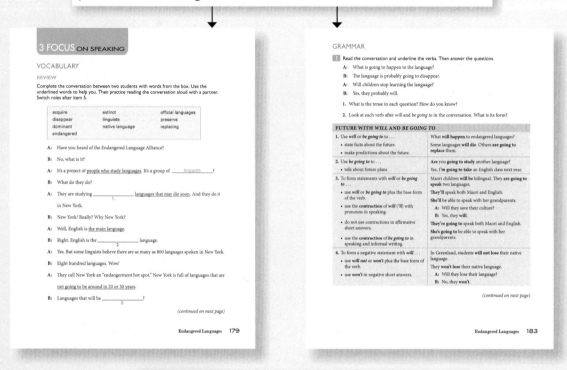

MyEnglishLab

Auto-graded vocabulary and grammar practice activities with feedback reinforce meaning, form, and function.

CT A final speaking task gives students an opportunity to exchange ideas and express opinions in sustained speaking contexts using the vocabulary, grammar, pronunciation, listening, and speaking skills presented in the unit.

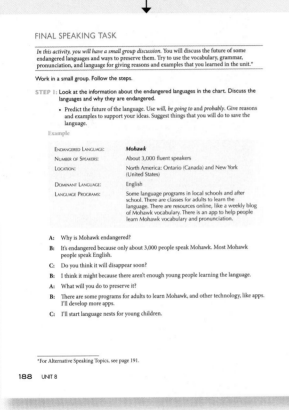

FINAL SPEAKING TASK

In this activity, you will have a small group discussion. You will discuss the future of some endangered languages and ways to preserve them. Try to use the vocabulary, grammar, pronunciation, and language for giving reasons and examples that you learned in the unit.*

Work in a small group. Follow the steps.

STEP 1: Look at the information about the endangered languages in the chart. Discuss the languages and why they are endangered.

- Predict the future of the language. Use *will*, *be going to* and *probably*. Give reasons and examples to support your ideas. Suggest things that you will do to save the language.

Example

ENDANGERED LANGUAGE:	**Mohawk**
NUMBER OF SPEAKERS:	About 3,000 fluent speakers
LOCATION:	North America: Ontario (Canada) and New York (United States)
DOMINANT LANGUAGE:	English
LANGUAGE PROGRAMS:	Some language programs in local schools and after school. There are classes for adults to learn the language. There are resources online, like a weekly blog of Mohawk vocabulary. There is an app to help people learn Mohawk vocabulary and pronunciation.

A: Why is Mohawk endangered?

B: It's endangered because only about 3,000 people speak Mohawk. Most Mohawk people speak English.

C: Do you think it will disappear soon?

B: I think it might because there aren't enough young people learning the language.

A: What will you do to preserve it?

B: There are some programs for adults to learn Mohawk, and other technology, like apps. I'll develop more apps.

C: I'll start language nests for young children.

---

*For Alternative Speaking Topics, see page 191.

188   UNIT 8

CT A group unit project inspires students to inquire further and prepares students to engage in real-world activities. Unit projects incorporate Internet research, helping to build students' digital literacy skills.

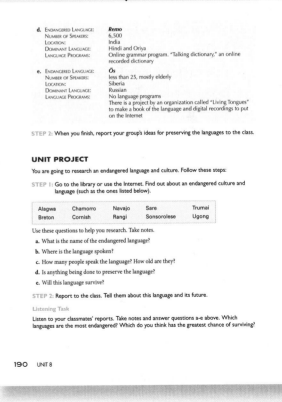

d.	ENDANGERED LANGUAGE:	**Remo**
	NUMBER OF SPEAKERS:	6,500
	LOCATION:	India
	DOMINANT LANGUAGE:	Hindi and Oriya
	LANGUAGE PROGRAMS:	Online grammar program. "Talking dictionary," an online recorded dictionary
e.	ENDANGERED LANGUAGE:	**Ös**
	NUMBER OF SPEAKERS:	less than 25, mostly elderly
	LOCATION:	Siberia
	DOMINANT LANGUAGE:	Russian
	LANGUAGE PROGRAMS:	No language programs
		There is a project by an organization called "Living Tongues" to make a book of the language and digital recordings to put on the Internet

STEP 2: When you finish, report your group's ideas for preserving the languages to the class.

UNIT PROJECT

You are going to research an endangered language and culture. Follow these steps:

STEP 1: Go to the library or use the Internet. Find out about an endangered culture and language (such as the ones listed below).

Alagwa	Chamorro	Navajo	Sare	Trumai
Breton	Cornish	Rangi	Sonsorolese	Ugong

Use these questions to help you research. Take notes.

a. What is the name of the endangered language?

b. Where is the language spoken?

c. How many people speak the language? How old are they?

d. Is anything being done to preserve the language?

e. Will this language survive?

STEP 2: Report to the class. Tell them about this language and its future.

Listening Task

Listen to your classmates' reports. Take notes and answer questions a-e above. Which languages are the most endangered? Which do you think has the greatest chance of surviving?

190   UNIT 8

Welcome to *NorthStar*   xi

INNOVATIVE TEACHING TOOLS

With instant access to a wide range of online content and diagnostic tools, teachers can customize learning environments to meet the needs of every student.

USING MyEnglishLab, NORTHSTAR TEACHERS CAN:

Deliver rich online content to engage and motivate students, including:

- student audio to support listening and speaking skills.
- engaging, authentic video clips, including reports adapted from ABC, NBC, and CBS newscasts, tied to the unit themes.
- opportunities for written and recorded reactions to be submitted by students.

Use a powerful selection of diagnostic reports to:

- view student scores by unit, skill, and activity.
- monitor student progress on any activity or test as often as needed.
- analyze class data to determine steps for remediation and support.

Use Teacher Resource eText* to access:

- a digital copy of the student book for whole class instruction.
- downloadable achievement and placement tests.
- printable resources, including lesson planners, videoscripts, and video activities.
- classroom audio.
- unit teaching notes and answer keys.

* Teacher Resource eText is accessible through MyEnglishLab: NorthStar.

COMPONENTS PRINT or eTEXT

STUDENT BOOK and MyEnglishLab

★ Student Book with MyEnglishLab

The two strands, Reading & Writing and Listening & Speaking, for each of the five levels, provide a fully blended approach with the seamless integration of print and online content.

eTEXT and MyEnglishLab

★ eText with MyEnglishLab

Offering maximum flexibility for different learning styles and needs, a digital version of the student book can be used on iPad® and Android® devices.

★ Instructor Access: Teacher Resource eText and MyEnglishLab (Listening & Speaking 1–5)

Teacher Resource eText

Each level and strand of *NorthStar* has an accompanying Teacher Resource eText that includes: a digital student book, unit teaching notes, answer keys, downloadable achievement tests, classroom audio, lesson planners, video activities, videoscripts, and a downloadable placement test.

MyEnglishLab

Teachers assign MyEnglishLab activities to reinforce the skills students learn in class and monitor progress through an online gradebook. The automatically graded exercises in MyEnglishLab *NorthStar* support and build on academic skills and vocabulary presented and practiced in the Student Book/eText. The teacher-graded activities include pronunciation, speaking, and writing, and are assigned by the instructor.

★ Classroom Audio CD

The Listening & Speaking audio contains the recordings and activities, as well as audio for the achievement tests. The Reading & Writing strand contains the readings on audio.

SCOPE AND SEQUENCE

UNIT OUTCOMES	1 WORK **OFFBEAT JOBS** pages 2–23 *Listening 1: What's My Job?* *Listening 2: More Offbeat Jobs*	2 STUDENT LIFE **WHERE DOES THE TIME GO?** pages 24–47 *Listening 1: Student Success Workshop* *Listening 2: A Student Discussion*
LISTENING	• Make and confirm predictions • Identify main ideas and details • Connect statements to specific speakers • Recognize connectors that compare and contrast ideas **MyEnglishLab** Vocabulary and Listening Skill Practice	• Make and confirm predictions • Identify main ideas and details • Connect statements to specific speakers • Recognize phrases that signal agreement and disagreement • Connect information from two listenings **MyEnglishLab** Vocabulary and Listening Skill Practice
SPEAKING	• Express opinions • Ask and answer questions about jobs, interests, and skills • Express interest • Express agreement and disagreement **Task:** Create and dramatize job interviews **MyEnglishLab** Speaking Skill Practice and Speaking Task	• Express opinions • Express various levels of agreement and disagreement • Support opinions with examples **Task:** Create, give, and report on a survey about student life **MyEnglishLab** Speaking Skill Practice and Speaking Task
INFERENCE	• Identify humor from a speaker's choice of words and tone	• Infer a speaker's intention based on questions the speaker asks
PRONUNCIATION	• Recognize syllable stress **MyEnglishLab** Pronunciation Skill Practice	• Recognize emphasis through intonation and stress **MyEnglishLab** Pronunciation Skill Practice
VOCABULARY	• Infer word meaning from context **MyEnglishLab** Vocabulary Practice	• Infer word meaning from context • Use familiar words to form collocations **MyEnglishLab** Vocabulary Practice
GRAMMAR	• Recognize and use descriptive adjectives **MyEnglishLab** Grammar Practice	• Recognize and use the present simple tense **MyEnglishLab** Grammar Practice
VIDEO	**MyEnglishLab** *Interview with a Skydiving Instructor,* Video Activity	**MyEnglishLab** *College Students Spark Creativity in Kids, Voice of America,* Video Activity
ASSESSMENTS	**MyEnglishLab** Check What You Know, Checkpoints 1 and 2, Unit 1 Achievement Test	**MyEnglishLab** Check What You Know, Checkpoints 1 and 2, Unit 2 Achievement Test

3 MONEY
A PENNY SAVED IS A PENNY EARNED
pages 48–71

Listening 1: A Barter Network
Listening 2: The Compact

4 ETIQUETTE
WHAT HAPPENED TO ETIQUETTE?
pages 72–93

Listening 1: Whatever Happened
to Manners?
Listening 2: Our Listeners Respond—
Why is there a lack of manners?

• Make and confirm predictions • Identify main ideas and details • Interpret a timeline • Recognize emphasis from intonation and stress • Categorize information from two listenings **MyEnglishLab** Vocabulary and Listening Skill Practice	• Make and confirm predictions • Identify main ideas and details • Recognize summary statements • Categorize reasons from two listenings **MyEnglishLab** Vocabulary and Listening Skill Practice
• Express agreement and disagreement • Compare products and services • Make and respond to suggestions **Task:** Negotiate for goods and services **MyEnglishLab** Speaking Skill Practice and Speaking Task	• Express opinions • Summarize key information • Support reasons with examples • Make and respond to requests and invitations **Task:** Create and dramatize a situation about manners **MyEnglishLab** Speaking Skill Practice and Speaking Task
• Infer a speaker's attitude from intonation and stress	• Infer contrasting ideas in statements from intonation and stress
• Recognize word stress in numbers and prices **MyEnglishLab** Pronunciation Skill Practice	• Recognize rising and falling intonation in questions and statements **MyEnglishLab** Pronunciation Skill Practice
• Infer word meaning from context **MyEnglishLab** Grammar Practice	• Infer word meaning from context • Recognize and use idioms **MyEnglishLab** Grammar Practice
• Recognize and use comparative adjectives **MyEnglishLab** Vocabulary Practice	• Recognize and use *can*, *could* and *would* in polite requests **MyEnglishLab** Vocabulary Practice
MyEnglishLab *The History of Money*, Video Activity	**MyEnglishLab** *How to Ask for a Date*, Video Activity
MyEnglishLab Check What You Know, Checkpoints 1 and 2, Unit 3 Achievement Test	**MyEnglishLab** Check What You Know, Checkpoints 1 and 2, Unit 4 Achievement Test

SCOPE AND SEQUENCE

UNIT OUTCOMES	5 FOOD THE FAT TAX pages 94–117 *Listening 1: The Nation Talks* *Listening 2: Listeners Call In*	6 HEROES EVERYDAY HEROES pages 118–141 *Listening 1: The Subway Hero* *Listening 2: Psychology Lecture—* *Altruism*
LISTENING	• Make and confirm predictions • Identify main ideas and details • Recognize language and intonation that signal clarification MyEnglishLab Vocabulary and Listening Skill Practice	• Make and confirm predictions • Identify main ideas and details • Take notes on a lecture • Recognize phrases that signal the organization and ideas in a lecture • Support general ideas in one listening with specific examples from a second listening MyEnglishLab Vocabulary and Listening Skill Practice
SPEAKING	• Express opinions and support them with reasons • Ask for and give advice • Ask for and provide clarification or repetition **Task:** Participate in a debate about the role of government in reducing obesity MyEnglishLab Speaking Skill Practice and Speaking Task	• Express opinions • Ask follow-up questions • Recognize and use signal phrases in presentations **Task:** Prepare and give a presentation MyEnglishLab Speaking Skill Practice and Speaking Task
INFERENCE	• Infer meaning by recognizing phrases that signal hedging	• Infer a speaker's feelings or emotion from tone of voice and word choice
PRONUNCIATION	• Recognize intonation in questions requesting clarification or repetition MyEnglishLab Pronunciation Skill Practice	• Recognize and pronounce the three -ed endings in the regular past tense MyEnglishLab Pronunciation Skill Practice
VOCABULARY	• Infer word meaning from context • Recognize and use words for healthy foods MyEnglishLab Vocabulary Practice	• Infer word meaning from context • Categorize words with similar meanings MyEnglishLab Vocabulary Practice
GRAMMAR	• Recognize and use modals of possibility (*may, might, could*) MyEnglishLab Grammar Practice	• Recognize and use the simple past tense MyEnglishLab Grammar Practice
VIDEO	MyEnglishLab *Food from the Hood*, Video Activity	MyEnglishLab *All for One*, ABC News, Video Activity
ASSESSMENTS	MyEnglishLab Check What You Know, Checkpoints 1 and 2, Unit 5 Achievement Test	MyEnglishLab Check What You Know, Checkpoints 1 and 2, Unit 6 Achievement Test

7 HEALTH
GAMING YOUR WAY TO BETTER HEALTH
pages 142–165

Listening 1: Gaming Your Way to Better Health
Listening 2: Technology in the Classroom

8 ENDANGERED CULTURES
ENDANGERED LANGUAGES
pages 166–191

Listening 1: Language Loss
Listening 2: My Life, My Language

• Make and confirm predictions • Identify main ideas and details • Recognize phrases and intonation that express doubt • Analyze advantages and disadvantages **MyEnglishLab** Vocabulary and Listening Skill Practice	• Make and confirm predictions • Identify main ideas and details • Interpret a graph • Recognize phrases that identify reasons and examples • Support ideas from one listening with examples from a second listening **MyEnglishLab** Vocabulary and Listening Skill Practice
• Express opinions • Give and respond to advice • Express concern **Task:** Prepare and present a TV commercial **MyEnglishLab** Speaking Skill Practice and Speaking Task	• Express opinions • Agree and disagree with opinions • Present and defend a position • Give reasons and examples to explain general statements **Task:** Participate in a small-group discussion **MyEnglishLab** Speaking Skill Practice and Speaking Task
• Infer a speaker's intended meaning from persuasive language	• Infer a speaker's viewpoint
• Recognize and produce reductions of modals **MyEnglishLab** Pronunciation Skill Practice	• Recognize and use contractions and reductions with *will* and *be going to* **MyEnglishLab** Pronunciation Skill Practice
• Infer word meaning from context **MyEnglishLab** Vocabulary Practice	• Infer word meaning from context • Recognize and use synonyms **MyEnglishLab** Vocabulary Practice
• Recognize and use modals of advice and necessity (*should, ought to, have to*) **MyEnglishLab** Grammar Practice	• Recognize and use the future with *will* and *be going to* **MyEnglishLab** Grammar Practice
MyEnglishLab *Chinese Medicine*, Video Activity	**MyEnglishLab** *Maori Culture*, Video Activity
MyEnglishLab Check What You Know, Checkpoints 1 and 2, Unit 7 Achievement Test	**MyEnglishLab** Check What You Know, Checkpoints 1 and 2, Unit 8 Achievement Test

ACKNOWLEDGMENTS

We would like to thank everyone at Pearson who helped us to make this new edition possible. Special thanks go to Debbie Sistino for her many years of guidance, support, and dedication to the success of *NorthStar*.

—*Laurie Frazier and Robin Mills*

REVIEWERS

Chris Antonellis, Boston University – CELOP; Gail August, Hostos; Aegina Barnes, York College; Kim Bayer, Hunter College; Mine Bellikli, Atilim University; Allison Blechman, Embassy CES; Paul Blomquist, Kaplan; Helena Botros, FLS; James Branchick, FLS; Chris Bruffee, Embassy CES; Nese Cakli, Duzce University; María Cordani Tourinho Dantas, Colégio Rainha De Paz; Jason Davis, ASC English; Lindsay Donigan, Fullerton College; Bina Dugan, BCCC; Sibel Ece Izmir, Atilim University; Érica Ferrer, Universidad del Norte; María Irma Gallegos Peláez, Universidad del Valle de México; Jeff Gano, ASA College; María Genovev a Chávez Bazán, Universidad del Valle de México; Juan Garcia, FLS; Heidi Gramlich, The New England School of English; Phillip Grayson, Kaplan; Rebecca Gross, The New England School of English; Rick Guadiana, FLS; Sebnem Guzel, Tobb University; Esra Hatipoglu, Ufuk University; Brian Henry, FLS; Josephine Horna, BCCC; Arthur Hui, Fullerton College; Zoe Isaacson, Hunter College; Kathy Johnson, Fullerton College; Marcelo Juica, Urban College of Boston; Tom Justice, North Shore Community College; Lisa Karakas, Berkeley College; Eva Kopernacki, Embassy CES; Drew Larimore, Kaplan; Heidi Lieb, BCCC; Patricia Martins, Ibeu; Cecilia Mora Espejo, Universidad del Valle de México; Kate Nyhan, The New England School of English; Julie Oni, FLS; Willard Osman, The New England School of English; Olga Pagieva, ASA College; Manish Patel, FLS; Paige Poole, Universidad del Norte; Claudia Rebello, Ibeu; Lourdes Rey, Universidad del Norte; Michelle Reynolds, FLS International Boston Commons; Mary Ritter, NYU; Minerva Santos, Hostos; Sezer Sarioz, Saint Benoit PLS; Ebru Sinar, Tobb University; Beth Soll, NYU (Columbia); Christopher Stobart, Universidad del Norte; Guliz Uludag, Ufuk University; Debra Un, NYU; Hilal Unlusu, Saint Benoit PLS; María del Carmen Viruega Trejo, Universidad del Valle de México; Reda Vural, Atilim University; Douglas Waters, Universidad del Norte; Leyla Yucklik, Duzce University; Jorge Zepeda Porras, Universidad del Valle de México

OFFBEAT Jobs

1. Look at the photo. What are the people doing? What is the man's job?

2. Read the title of the unit. *Offbeat* means unusual. A bike messenger has an offbeat job. Can you think of other offbeat jobs?

3. What is most important to you when choosing a job? Think about things like salary (how much money you make), hours, interest, safety (how safe or dangerous it is), workplace (indoors, outdoors, home, office), education, and number of job openings (how easy it is to find a job). Compare your answers as a class.

GO TO MyEnglishLab TO CHECK WHAT YOU KNOW.

2 FOCUS ON LISTENING

VOCABULARY

1 🎧 Read and listen to the job postings on a website for college students.

● ○ ○	
HOME **CONTACT** **ABOUT US**	Looking for a fun summer job? Need to earn some extra **income**? Here are some jobs you might like. Visit the College Job Center office for more information about these jobs.

Bike Messenger	**Computer Assembler**	**Insurance Salesperson**
Do you like exciting and sometimes dangerous activities? Do you like to work outdoors? Are you athletic? Then this offbeat job is just for you. For this job, you must have your own bike and be able to ride quickly through the city to deliver packages and letters to our customers.	Do you like computers? Do you know a lot about them? We need people to work in our **factory** to make computers. You must be fast and like to build things. You must also be able to **concentrate** so you put the parts together correctly without making mistakes.	Do you like sales? Do you like to work with people? Come work in our insurance company. We sell every kind of **insurance policy**: auto, home, life, and medical.
Computer Animation Artist	**Restaurant Blogger**	**Professional Secret Shopper**
Are you artistic? Are you good with computers? Do you like to play video and computer games? Then we have the right job for you. Our video game company makes games that are popular with many generations of people, from children to adults of all ages. We are looking for young **creative** people to help us make some new games for the next **generation** of game players.	Do you like good food and eating out in restaurants? Are you a good writer? Then we need you! For this job, you will need to **taste** different kinds of food—even spicy food, such as Thai or Mexican. You also need a good sense of taste. Your **tongue** must be able to taste many different **flavors**, such as sweet or sour, so you can write about the foods you try.	Do you like to shop, but you don't like to spend money? You can be a **professional** shopper and get paid to shop! Our stores hire secret shoppers to make sure the salespeople are doing a good job.

---

2 Match the words on the left with the definitions on the right.

_d_ **1.** concentrate

a. thinking of new ways of doing things

____ **2.** factory

b. an agreement with an insurance company to be paid money in case of an accident, illness, or death

____ **3.** insurance policy

c. all the people who are about the same age

____ **4.** creative

~~**d.** to be careful and pay attention~~

____ **5.** income

e. a building where things are made

____ **6.** taste

f. the part inside your mouth that moves and is used for eating food and speaking

____ **7.** professional

____ **8.** flavor

g. particular taste of a food or drink

____ **9.** generation

h. doing something for money instead of for fun or pleasure

____ **10.** tongue

i. try food by eating a little bit

j. the money you earn when you work

■■■■■■■■■■■■■■■■■■■■■■■■■■■■■■■■■■■■ GO TO MyEnglishLab FOR MORE VOCABULARY PRACTICE.

PREVIEW

1 🎧 People can have many different kinds of jobs. Some are usual and some are offbeat.

Listen to the beginning of *What's My Job?* Circle the correct answer to complete each statement.

1. You are listening to a ____.

    a. job interview   **b.** game show   **c.** radio show

2. Wayne is a ____.

    a. host   **b.** contestant   **c.** guest

(continued on next page)

3. Rita is a _____.

    a. host   **b.** contestant   **c.** guest

4. Peter is going to describe _____.

    a. his job   **b.** his company   **c.** himself

2 Make predictions. Circle more than one answer.

Peter will talk about . . .

    a. what he does.   **c.** how much money he makes.   **e.** what he likes to do.

    b. where he works.   **d.** what he is like.

MAIN IDEAS

1 🎧 Listen to *What's My Job?* Look at your predictions from the Preview section. Were any of them correct? Did your predictions help you understand the listening?

2 Circle the correct answer to complete each statement.

1. Rita asks Peter questions to guess _____.

    a. his last name   **b.** his job   **c.** his age

2. Peter works in a _____.

    a. restaurant   **b.** factory   **c.** bakery

3. Peter is _____.

    a. a factory worker   **b.** a chef   **c.** an ice-cream taster

4. Peter has to be careful with _____.

    a. his taste buds   **b.** the ice cream   **c.** the factory machines

5. Peter thinks his job is _____.

    a. tiring   **b.** great   **c.** dangerous

DETAILS

🎧 Listen to *What's My Job?* again. Then read each statement. Write **T** *(true)* or **F** *(false)*. Correct the false statements.

_____ **1.** Peter can be creative at work.

_____ **2.** Peter thinks of new ice-cream flavors.

_____ **3.** He eats all the ice cream at work.

_____ **4.** He doesn't eat spicy foods.

_____ **5.** He doesn't drink alcohol or coffee.

_____ **6.** He smokes.

_____ **7.** He has a one-million-dollar insurance policy on his taste buds.

_____ **8.** He studied ice-cream tasting in school.

■■■■■■■■■■■■■■■■■■■■■■■■■■■■■■■■■■■■■■ *GO TO* MyEnglishLab *FOR MORE LISTENING PRACTICE.*

MAKE INFERENCES

UNDERSTANDING THE USE OF HUMOR

An inference is a guess about something that is not directly stated. To make an inference, use information that you understand from what you hear.

Usually speakers use words to express their true meaning, but sometimes speakers want to be funny or humorous. We can often tell when people are using humor when they use words we don't expect. Their words may be surprising, or they may express the opposite of what they mean. We can also tell when people are using humor when they laugh or use a humorous sound in their voice.

🎧 Listen to the example. Listen to the words and the tone of voice. Is the speaker expressing his true meaning, or is he using humor? What words or tone can you hear that tell you the speaker's meaning?

Example

HOST: Gee, sounds like a difficult job, Peter. You taste ice cream all day, and you get paid for it!

    a. true meaning

    b. humor

In the example, the speaker uses the word *difficult* to describe Peter's job, but the words he uses in the next sentence show that he really thinks it is easy to be an ice-cream taster. He just says it is *difficult* in order to be humorous. You can also hear from his tone that he is using humor.

🎧 Listen to the excerpts. Is Wayne expressing his true meaning or is he using humor? Circle the correct word.

Excerpt One

    Wow! You do have to be careful.

    a. true meaning

    b. humor

Excerpt Two

    1. *Gee, you do have an important job, Peter.*

    a. true meaning

    b. humor

    2. *Did you go to ice-cream tasting school?*

    a. true meaning

    b. humor

EXPRESS OPINIONS

Work in a small group. Discuss the questions. Explain your opinions.

1. Do you think Peter's job is difficult or easy? Why do you think so?

2. Do you think you could do Peter's job? Why or why not?

3. Do you think it was easy for Peter to get started in his job? Why or why not?

■■■■■■■■■■■■■■■■■■■■■■■■■■ *GO TO* MyEnglishLab *TO GIVE YOUR OPINION ABOUT ANOTHER QUESTION.*

LISTENING TWO A CONVERSATION WITH A JOB COUNSELOR

VOCABULARY

Read the words in the box aloud. Then read the sentences and circle the letter of the answer that shows the correct definition of the boldfaced word.

career	quit	relaxing	stressful	tiring

1. In my opinion, the most **relaxing** thing to do after a long day at work is to sit in my favorite chair and watch TV.

    a. helping you to rest   **b.** helping you to work hard

2. I am studying computer animation in school. I want to have a **career** making animated movies.

    a. something you study in school   **b.** a kind of work you do for a long time

3. I am unhappy at my job. I think I will **quit** and find a new job.

    a. leave a job   **b.** continue working at a job

4. I stand on my feet all day assembling computers. I wish I could sit down. It is very **tiring**.

    a. causing you to stand   **b.** causing you to feel sleepy

5. Tests are very **stressful** for me; I am afraid I won't do well.

    a. causing you to feel worried   **b.** difficult

■■■■■■■■■■■■■■■■■■■■■■■■■■■■■■■■■■ *GO TO* MyEnglishLab *FOR MORE VOCABULARY PRACTICE.*

COMPREHENSION

You will listen to two people talking with a job counselor about their jobs. A job counselor is someone who helps people find the right job or career. One person is a window washer. The other person is a professional shopper. The job counselor is helping them choose new careers.

🎧 **Listen to the conversation. Then look at the statements in the chart. Put a check (✓) in the correct column for the window washer or the professional shopper. Some statements may be true for both.**

	WINDOW WASHER	PROFESSIONAL SHOPPER
a. I like my job.		
b. I work outdoors.		
c. I earn a high salary.		
d. My work is dangerous.		
e. I like to work with people.		
f. I'm good with money.		
g. I'm good with my hands.		
h. My work is tiring.		
i. It was difficult to get started in this job.		
j. I have my own business.		
k. I want to quit and find a new job.		
l. I don't want to be the boss.		
m. I like working for myself.		

LISTENING SKILL

NOTICING CONTRAST

But and *however* are connectors that introduce a clause with an idea, opinion, or action that is different from the first idea. They show a contrast.

🎧 Listen to the example. Note the contrast word.

Example

The speaker is contrasting two ideas:

Idea 1: it was difficult to get started.

Idea 2: He started his own business. He likes working for himself.

He uses *but* to connect the two ideas.

🎧 Listen to the excerpts. The speaker contrasts two ideas. What are they? What connector does she use to show the difference?

Excerpt One

> **Idea 1:** I love _____ and I like _____.
>
> I'm very good _____.
>
> **Idea 2:** My job _____.
>
> I'm _____, so my work _____.
>
> What word does she use to show the difference? _____

Excerpt Two

> **Idea 1:** I _____ my job and _____.
>
> I like _____.
>
> **Idea 2:** I have to _____ and _____.
>
> What word does she use to show the difference? _____

▪▪▪▪▪▪▪▪▪▪▪▪▪▪▪▪▪▪▪▪▪▪▪▪▪▪▪▪▪▪▪ *GO TO* MyEnglishLab *FOR MORE SKILL PRACTICE.*

STEP 1: Organize

🎧 Listen to the excerpts. Read the questions a person might ask about these three unusual jobs. Then answer the questions with the information from Listenings One and Two.

	WINDOW WASHER	PROFESSIONAL SHOPPER	ICE-CREAM TASTER
1. Can you describe what you do?	I wash office building windows.		
2. What do you like about your job?		I love to shop.	
3. What's difficult about your job?			I can't eat the ice cream. I have to take care of my taste buds. I can't eat spicy food.
4. What skills do you need to do your job?			

Compare your answers with a partner's. Discuss any differences.

STEP 2: Synthesize

Work with a partner. Student A, you are a host on a radio show. You are interviewing people about their unusual jobs. Student B, you are a guest on the show. You are talking about your offbeat job. Use the questions and the information from Step 1 to guide your conversation.

Example

A: What is your job?

B: I'm a window washer.

A: Can you describe what you do?

B: I wash office building windows. I go high up in a basket to reach the windows.

Switch roles and talk about a different job from Step 1.

GO TO MyEnglishLab TO CHECK WHAT YOU LEARNED.

VOCABULARY

REVIEW

Match the statement on the left with the best response on the right.

__b__ 1. My friend went to school to learn to cook. She just got her first job cooking in a French restaurant. She loves her job.

_____ 2. Working for myself isn't easy. I have a lot of work to do.

_____ 3. I don't like my job. I want to get a new job.

_____ 4. I need to work where it is very quiet. I have to pay very close attention so I don't make any mistakes.

_____ 5. I love making up stories. Someday I want to write my own book.

_____ 6. I want to be a doctor. I know I need to be in school for a long time, but being a doctor is my dream.

_____ 7. I worked really hard all week, so last weekend I just stayed home and watched movies.

_____ 8. I think walking dogs for a job is fun. The only problem is that all the walking is a lot of work!

a. It sounds like you want to **quit**!

b. ~~You're so lucky your friend is a professional chef! Does she ever cook for you?~~

c. Wow, having your own business sounds really **stressful**.

d. You are very **creative**.

e. That sounds very **relaxing**!

f. If that's really what you want to do, I think it's a **career** you will enjoy.

g. Yes, it is a very **tiring** job.

h. You really need to **concentrate**.

Work with a partner. Read the sentences below. Circle the best definition for each boldfaced word or phrase.

1. I work 60 hours a week, and I always think about my work. I am a **workaholic**.

   A workaholic is a person who _____.

   a. works a lot and finds it difficult not to work   **b.** knows a lot of people

2. I want a career where I can work with money. I am very **good with numbers**.

   Someone who is good with numbers _____.

   a. likes to count and do math   **b.** doesn't like doing math

3. I want to be a professional shopper because **I don't want to have a boss**.

   If I don't want to have a boss, I want to _____.

   a. work for myself   **b.** work in a big company

4. Some people like office jobs. Not me. I enjoy a job that lets me make things. I am **good with my hands**.

   A person who is good with his or her hands _____.

   a. likes to do office work all day   **b.** is good at fixing or building things

5. I'm good at finding solutions to difficult situations. My friends often ask me to help them. They say I am a good **problem solver**.

   A problem solver _____.

   a. is good at finding the best way to do something   **b.** needs a lot of help doing things

6. I really enjoy working in a store because I like talking to and helping people. I have **good people skills**.

   Someone with good people skills _____.

   a. can relate well with other people   **b.** is usually very shy

7. I am good at telling people what I think, and I can explain things well. I am very clear when I speak. I have **good communication skills**.

A person with good communication skills _____.

   a. is difficult to understand

   b. is very easy to understand

8. I always come to work on time and do my work well. Sometimes I stay longer at work to finish my job. My boss says I'm **hardworking**.

A hardworking person _____.

   a. works a lot and is not lazy

   b. doesn't do a good job

9. My favorite job was working in a restaurant. There were many people working there, and we worked well together. We were all **team players**.

A team player _____.

   a. works alone and doesn't help others

   b. works in a group and helps others

10. I worked in a store last year. The boss let me count the money at the end of the day and take it to the bank. My boss didn't worry because I am **trustworthy**.

A trustworthy person is _____.

   a. honest

   b. not honest

11. I really enjoy working as a dog walker. I don't have to sit indoors at a desk. I can work **outdoors** in the fresh air and sunshine.

A job that is outdoors is _____

   a. not a desk job

   b. inside a building

12. I think being up high washing windows is very exciting, but it's important to be careful so you don't fall or have an accident. If you are not careful, it can be very **dangerous**.

A dangerous job is not _____.

   a. exciting

   b. safe

Work with a partner. Look at the words in the box. Can you add any other words that you might use in a job interview? Practice asking and answering the questions. Use the words from the box and vocabulary from Review and Expand in your answers.

Skills: Talents or abilities	Characteristics: Your strengths (strong points) and weaknesses (weak points)	Types of jobs
be good with numbers	friendly	indoors
be good with my hands	creative	outdoors
have good people skills	hardworking	safe
have good communication skills	trustworthy	dangerous
_____	a team player	high-paying
_____	a problem solver	offbeat
_____	a workaholic	stressful
	_____	relaxing
	_____	tiring
	_____	_____
		_____
		_____

1. Tell me about yourself. What do you do now? What kind of person are you? Give an example.

    I am _____.

    _____.

2. What type of job do you want?

    I'd like _____

    _____.

3. What skills do you have? Give an example of when you used that skill.

    I _____.

    I _____.

4. What are your strengths? Give an example.

I _____.

I _____.

5. What are your weaknesses? Give an example.

I _____.

I _____.

■■■■■■■■■■■■■■■■■■■■■■■■■■■■■■■■■■ GO TO MyEnglishLab *FOR MORE VOCABULARY PRACTICE.*

GRAMMAR

1 Work with a partner. Read the conversations aloud. Look at the underlined words. Then answer the questions.

1. **A:** What's your job like?
   B: My job is <u>interesting</u>.

2. **A:** What kind of person are you?
   B: I'm a <u>friendly</u> person.

a. Look at the answers to the questions. What is the verb in each sentence?

b. What is the noun in each sentence?

c. Which words describe the nouns? Where do they come in the sentences?

DESCRIPTIVE ADJECTIVES	
Adjectives describe nouns.	
1. Adjectives can come after the verb *be.*	My job **is *tiring*.**
2. Adjectives can also come before a noun.	Artists are ***creative* people.**
3. When a singular noun follows an adjective, use *a* before the adjective if the adjective begins with a consonant sound.	This isn't **a *high-paying* job.**
4. When a singular noun follows an adjective, use *an* before the adjective if the adjective begins with a vowel sound.	Peter has **an *offbeat* job.**

2 Some words describe a person, some describe a job, and some describe both. Write the words in the correct box.

boring	dangerous	friendly	hardworking	interesting	relaxing	tiring
creative	difficult	happy	high-paying	offbeat	safe	

WORDS ABOUT PEOPLE	WORDS ABOUT JOBS	WORDS ABOUT BOTH

3 Work with a partner. Take turns making statements using the nouns and adjectives provided. After one of you makes a statement, the other one reacts, saying, "I agree" or "I don't agree." If you don't agree with a statement, correct it.

Example

A restaurant blogger's work / dangerous

A: A restaurant blogger's work is dangerous.

B: I don't agree. A restaurant blogger's work isn't dangerous. It's safe.

1. a bike messenger's job / tiring

2. an ice-cream taster / creative person

3. an insurance salesperson's work / stressful

4. computer animation /offbeat job

5. window washing / interesting job

6. a game show host / hardworking

7. a professional shopper's job / relaxing

GO TO MyEnglishLab FOR MORE GRAMMAR PRACTICE.

PRONUNCIATION

STRESS

In words with multiple syllables, one syllable is stressed. Stressed syllables sound longer than unstressed syllables. They are also louder and higher in pitch than unstressed syllables.

🎧 Listen to the examples.

careful

creative

generation

A compound noun is formed when two nouns are used together as one noun. In compound nouns, the stress is stronger on the first word in the compound.

🎧 Listen to the examples.

bike messenger

sales clerk

When an adjective is followed by a noun, the stress is usually stronger on the noun.

🎧 Listen to the examples.

professional shopper

good pay

1 🎧 Listen to the adjectives. Write the number of syllables you hear in each adjective. Then listen again and underline the stressed syllable. Listen a third time and repeat the words.

_____ 1. dangerous

_____ 2. important

_____ 3. tiring

_____ 4. educated

_____ 5. difficult

_____ 6. spicy

_____ 7. unusual

_____ 8. interesting

2 🎧 Read each item and underline the stressed syllable. Next, listen to check your answers. Then work with a partner. Take turns saying each item and listening for the correct stress.

1. animation artist

2. window washer

3. high salary

4. computer assembler

5. ice cream

6. spicy foods

7. department store

3 Work with a partner. Student A, ask *Wh-* questions with the phrases on the left. Student B, answer with the phrases on the right. Be sure to use the correct stress. Switch roles after item 4. Write your answers on the lines.

Example

A: What do you call someone who washes windows?

B: A window washer.

_b_ **1.** someone who washes windows		**a.** bike messenger
____ **2.** a frozen dessert		**b.** ~~window washer~~
____ **3.** someone who sells things		**c.** job counselor
____ **4.** someone who makes animated movies or games		**d.** animation artist
____ **5.** a large store that sells many different products		**e.** ice cream
____ **6.** someone who puts together computers		**f.** department store
____ **7.** a person who delivers letters and packages by bike		**g.** computer assembler
____ **8.** someone who helps people find the right job or career		**h.** salesclerk

SPEAKING SKILL

MAKING CONVERSATION

When making conversation, it's polite to ask about a person's job and interests (what people like to do in their free time). It's also polite to express interest (to react positively) when people tell you something about themselves.

Asking About Someone's Job and Interests	Talking About Yourself	Showing Interest
What do you do?	I'm not working right now. I'm a (student / chef / homemaker). I'm retired.[1]	Oh . . . really?
How do you like it?	It's great. It's interesting. It's all right, but . . . I don't like it at all.	Good for you. Oh, I see. Oh, why not?
What do you like to do in your free time?	I like to (listen to music / play tennis). I enjoy (reading / playing computer games).	That's interesting. That's nice. Really? Me, too! Oh, yeah?

Work with a partner. Complete the conversation with your own information. Then practice it aloud.

A: Hi. My name's _____.

B: Hi. I'm _____. Nice to meet you.

A: Nice to meet you, too. So what do you do?

B: I'm _____.

A: _____. How do you like it?

B: _____. How about you? What do you do?

A: _____.

B: _____. So what do you like to do in your free time?

A: _____. How about you?

B: _____.

---

[1] **retired:** no longer working at a job, usually because of age

■■■■■■■■■■■■■■■■ *GO TO* MyEnglishLab *FOR MORE SKILL PRACTICE AND TO CHECK WHAT YOU LEARNED.*

FINAL SPEAKING TASK

In this activity, you will take part in a workshop for people looking for jobs. In the workshop, people with offbeat jobs want to get different jobs. Job counselors talk with them to identify their skills and think of new jobs. Try to use the vocabulary, grammar, pronunciation, and language to make small talk that you learned in the unit.*

Follow the steps.

STEP 1: Divide into two groups.

Group A: people with offbeat jobs who want to change jobs

Group B: job counselors, who can help identify skills and new jobs

Group A: Each student chooses one job from the list below or another offbeat job. This is the job you now have. List the skills, characteristics, and strengths a person needs to do that job. Use words like: *creative, good with numbers,* and *trustworthy.* Then list reasons why you want to find a new job.

animation artist   restaurant blogger

game show host   window washer

ice-cream taster   other: _____

professional shopper

Group B: Write five questions to ask the job holders.

Examples

What skills do you have?

Why do you want to change jobs?

STEP 2: Form new groups. Half of each new group is from group A, half from group B. Offbeat job holders (Group A) sit in a line facing the job counselors (Group B).

Conduct a workshop:

- Each job holder briefly introduces himself or herself and then gives a short talk about his or her current job.

- Each counselor asks one or two questions to each job holder.

STEP 3: To end the workshop, each job counselor names a new job that might be good for the job holders. Explain which skills the job holders can use in their new jobs.

---

*For Alternative Speaking Topics, see page 23.

UNIT PROJECT

Would you like to find an offbeat job? Follow these steps:

STEP 1: Work in small groups. Brainstorm some offbeat jobs and make a list. You can include jobs from the unit or other offbeat jobs that you know.

STEP 2: Now, work alone. Choose one offbeat job you would like to have. Go to the library, look on the Internet, or interview someone who does the job to get information about it. Take notes. Your notes should include this information:

Job title: **Workplace:**

_____   _____

Person has to be:

_____

Person has to like:

_____

Why the job is interesting:

_____

STEP 3: Report your information to the class.

Listening Task

Listen to your classmates' reports. Which job do you think is the most interesting?

ALTERNATIVE SPEAKING TOPICS

Discuss the questions. Use the vocabulary and grammar from the unit.

1. Why do you think some people like offbeat jobs?

2. How do you think people get started in their offbeat jobs in the first place?

3. What job skills do you think are the most difficult to learn? Why do you think they are difficult?

4. What skills do you think are most important for students to learn so they can find a job or start a career in the future?

GO TO MyEnglishLab TO DISCUSS ONE OF THE ALTERNATIVE TOPICS, WATCH A VIDEO ABOUT AN OFFBEAT JOB, AND TAKE THE UNIT 1 ACHIEVEMENT TEST.

WHERE DOES THE
Time Go?

1. Look at the photo. Which of these activities do you think the student is doing: Doing school work, listening to music, texting (sending a written message by phone), chatting online (having a conversation), surfing the Web (looking at different Internet sites), watching videos, playing video games? Do you ever do any of these activities at the same time? Which ones?

2. *Challenges* are things that are difficult to do. What are some challenges that students face? What are some challenges you face as a student?

3. Read the title of the unit. What do you think this expression means? When do people say this?

GO TO MyEnglishLab TO CHECK WHAT YOU KNOW.

VOCABULARY

1 🎧 Read and listen to the college website about a student workshop.

City College Counseling Center
Student Success[1] Workshop

- Do you feel like you don't have enough time to finish all of your daily **tasks** and assignments?

- Do you spend a lot of time studying but still get poor grades?

- Do you have trouble concentrating in classes and lectures?

- Do you delay doing your school work and **put off** your assignments until just before they are due?

If you answered "yes" to any of these questions, then this College Success Workshop is for you!

There are many **factors** that lead to student success, such as choosing the right classes, having good study skills, getting help from teachers and counselors, and staying healthy and active. Another important factor is time management. Many students don't know how to **manage** their time well. For example, do you try to multitask or do other activities when you study, such as text messaging friends while you do homework? You may think you are saving time, but in fact multitasking has a **negative** effect on your ability to think and learn. Many **research studies** show that our brains are not able to concentrate on more than one challenging task at a time. Studies also show that students who multitask do worse in school than students who don't. They take more time to finish their work, and they receive lower test scores and grades.

Another big problem for students is **procrastination**. Do you have a hard time getting started on assignments? Do you **avoid** your schoolwork by doing other activities instead? Or maybe you quit working on assignments when you don't know how to finish. Then you are a procrastinator. Procrastinators avoid doing the things they should be doing now, saying they will do them later.

But don't worry. We are here to help. In our one-day workshop, we will give you **strategies** to help you:

- set **goals** and organize the tasks you need to get done

- learn better study habits

- avoid **distractions** that keep you from getting your work done

- stop procrastinating and get things done on time

Don't put it off any longer! Sign up in the counseling office today. College success will be your **reward**!

---

[1] **success:** being able to do what you tried to do or want to do

2 Match each boldfaced word or phrase in the text with its definition or synonym.

_h_ **1.** tasks

a. something you want to do in the future

_____ **2.** put off

b. things that make it difficult to think or pay attention

_____ **3.** factors

c. something that is given for doing good work

_____ **4.** manage

d. harmful or bad

_____ **5.** negative

e. to have control of something

_____ **6.** research studies

f. plans or ways to get something done

_____ **7.** procrastination

g. to delay something

_____ **8.** avoid

h. jobs or pieces of work that must be done

_____ **9.** strategies

i. things that cause a situation

_____ **10.** goals

j. careful study to report new knowledge about something

_____ **11.** distractions

k. to delay doing something that you should do, usually because you do not want to do it

_____ **12.** reward

l. to choose not to do something or to stay away from someone or something

GO TO MyEnglishLab FOR MORE VOCABULARY PRACTICE.

PREVIEW

A college counselor welcomes new students to a workshop on time management for college success.

🎧 Listen to the beginning of a student success workshop. What strategies do you think the counselor will suggest?

1. _____

2. _____

3. _____

MAIN IDEAS

1 🎧 Listen to the whole workshop. Look again at your predictions from the Preview section. How did your predictions help you understand the listening?

2 🎧 Listen and check (✓) the strategies that the counselor suggests.

_____ **1.** Set goals and write down all of the tasks you need to do.

_____ **2.** Put your list of goals in order.

_____ **3.** Review your class notes every day.

_____ **4.** Use a calendar to schedule your time.

_____ **5.** Divide big assignments into smaller tasks.

_____ **6.** When school is stressful, take a lot of breaks.

_____ **7.** Avoid distractions.

_____ **8.** Join a study group.

_____ **9.** Reward yourself for finishing your work on time.

DETAILS

Listen to the workshop again. Circle the best answer to complete each statement.

1. _____ of the students in the workshop like to multitask while they study.

    a. A few

    b. A lot

    c. All

2. _____ percent of students procrastinate sometimes.

    a. 20–35

    b. 70–85

    c. 80–95

3. The counselor suggests that you number your goals from _____.

    a. most important to least important

    b. most difficult to least difficult

    c. biggest to smallest

4. The counselor suggests that you schedule things like _____.

    a. exercising, taking naps, and seeing movies

    b. exercising, getting enough sleep, and seeing friends

    c. eating, doing homework, and taking breaks

5. The counselor thinks you should _____ to get your work done.

    a. find the strategies that work best for you

    b. always use the "Do Nothing" strategy

    c. do your English paper all at once

(continued on next page)

6. With the "Do Nothing" strategy, you can _____.

    a. do your work or do nothing

    b. get distracted or do nothing

    c. turn off your phone or do nothing

7. _____ is NOT a way to remove distractions.

    a. Putting away your video games

    b. Turning off your Internet

    c. Reading but not answering your text messages

8. Piers Steele took _____ to finish his research on procrastination.

    a. 2 years

    b. 10 years

    c. 20 years

9. Piers Steele suggests giving away _____ if you don't get your work done.

    a. some money

    b. your phone

    c. your video games

GO TO MyEnglishLab FOR MORE LISTENING PRACTICE.

MAKE INFERENCES

UNDERSTANDING QUESTIONS

An inference is an educated guess about something that is not directly stated in the text. To make an inference, use information that you understand from what you hear.

Speakers often ask questions when they are teaching or presenting information. This is a way to get our attention and involve us in the presentation. Sometimes we need to guess when a speaker wants responses to a question and when a speaker wants us to just listen for the answer. When speakers want us to respond, they may use phrases to signal that they want a response. They also pause and wait for us to answer the question or raise our hands.

🎧 Read and listen to the example. How do you know the speaker wants a response?

Example 1

> So, how many of you like to multitask—you know, like surf the Web or chat with your friends while you study? (pause). . . . OK . . . I see a lot of you . . .

In this example, the speaker signals the question by saying "So how many of you . . ." She also pauses and waits for the students to respond.

However, sometimes speakers just want us to pay attention and think about the answer to a question. In this case, speakers don't wait long enough for us to respond. Instead, they answer the questions themselves.

🎧 Read and listen to this example.

Example 2

> And be careful with big assignments—like that English paper—you can't do it all at once, right? No, you need to divide it into smaller tasks that you can do one at a time.

In this example, the speaker doesn't wait for responses. She just wants us to think about the answer, but then he answers the question himself.

🎧 Listen to three excerpts from the workshop. Does the speaker want the students to respond? How do you know? Circle the correct answer.

Excerpt One

The speaker _____.

a. wants a response

b. doesn't want a response

How do you know?

a. The speaker uses signal phrases to invite a response.

b. The speaker doesn't use signal phrases to invite a response.

a. The speaker waits for a response.

b. The speaker doesn't wait for a response.

(continued on next page)

The speaker _____.

a. wants a response

b. doesn't want a response

How do you know?

a. The speaker uses signal phrases to invite a response.

b. The speaker doesn't use signal phrases to invite a response.

a. The speaker waits for a response.

b. The speaker doesn't wait for a response.

The speaker _____.

a. wants a response

b. doesn't want a response

How do you know?

a. The speaker uses signal phrases to invite a response.

b. The speaker doesn't use signal phrases to invite a response.

a. The speaker waits for a response.

b. The speaker doesn't wait for a response.

EXPRESS OPINIONS

Discuss the questions with the class.

1. The speaker says that multitasking has a negative effect on students' ability to study. Do you agree? Why or why not?

2. What do you think is the main reason that students procrastinate? Is there ever a good reason to procrastinate?

3. Do you think that the strategies mentioned by the counselor are a good idea? Are there any you would never try? Why or why not? What other strategies do you use?

■■■■■■■■■■■■■■■■■■■■■■■■■■■ *GO TO* MyEnglishLab *TO GIVE YOUR OPINION ABOUT ANOTHER QUESTION.*

VOCABULARY

Read the words in the box. Then read the statements. Circle the best definition for the word or phrase in bold.

achieve	focus	positive attitude	pressure	waste

1. Anita wants to graduate from college. She is hardworking, so I'm sure she will **achieve** her goal.

   a. to want to do something

   b. to get something by working hard

2. When you are in class, it's important to **focus** on what the teacher is saying. You should pay attention so you can remember the important points.

   a. to direct your attention or effort

   b. to remember what someone told you

3. This history class is very challenging, but I have a **positive attitude**, and I think that I can do well if I work hard.

   a. a hardworking person

   b. a hopeful way of thinking

4. At my school, there is a lot of **pressure** to get good grades. Some parents and teachers even expect you to get straight A's.

   a. getting good grades in school

   b. feeling of stress because people expect you to do something

5. My roommate **wastes** a lot of time talking on the phone when she should be doing her homework. Then she never has enough time to finish.

   a. to use something in a way that is not useful or effective

   b. to do something quickly

■■■■■■■■■■■■■■■■■■■■■■■■■■■■■■■■■ GO TO MyEnglishLab FOR MORE VOCABULARY PRACTICE.

COMPREHENSION

🎧 You will listen to a group of students having a discussion in the college success workshop.

Read the statements. Put a check (✓) in the correct column for Annie, Sam, and Justin. Some statements may be true for more than one student

	ANNIE	SAM	JUSTIN
a. My grades aren't very good.			
b. I want to go to medical school.			
c. My parents pressure me to get straight A's			
d. I multitask while I'm studying or in class.			
e. I listen to music and chat with friends while I study.			
f. I surf the Web while I'm working on the computer.			
g. Sometimes it's hard for me to focus in class.			
h. I don't think multitasking is so bad for you.			
i. I put off assignments that are hard.			
j. I put off assignments I don't like to do.			
k. It's important to me to achieve my goals.			
l. I want to set goals and schedule my time better.			
m. I plan to put my phone away during class.			
n. I plan to give myself rewards for getting my work done.			

LISTENING SKILL

UNDERSTANDING DISAGREEMENT

Speakers use different phrases to disagree with each other's opinions. To disagree politely, speakers usually avoid saying "I disagree with you" directly. Instead, they use other phrases to disagree and then give a different opinion.

🎧 Read and listen to this example.

Example

A: My counselor said this workshop would help, but I don't know. I think we're wasting our time.

B: Really? You think so? I hope it's going to be useful. I want to go to medical school, so it's really important for me to do well in school.

In this example, the first speaker expresses his disagreement with the counselor's opinion by saying "I don't know." This is a polite way to say "I disagree" or "I have a different opinion." The second speaker disagrees by saying "Really?" Then she gives a different opinion.

🎧 Listen to excerpts from *A Student Discussion*. Write the phrase the second speaker uses to disagree. Then write the speaker's different opinion.

Excerpt One

Phrase to disagree: _____

Different opinion: _____

Excerpt Two

Phrase to disagree: _____

Different opinion: _____

■■ *GO TO* MyEnglishLab *FOR MORE SKILL PRACTICE.*

STEP 1: Organize

Complete the chart with the statements about the bad study habits of the students in Listening Two. Then write the strategies from Listening One that the students could use to improve their study habits. Some of the answers are done for you.

Try the "Do Nothing" Strategy

Text friends during class.

Divide big assignments into smaller tasks

Listen to music and chat online while doing homework.

Give yourself rewards for finishing your work.

~~Remove distractions, such as phones, games, Internet~~

~~Waste time playing video games instead of studying~~

~~Set goals and put them in order of importance~~

Put off assignments that you don't like to do.

Use a calendar to plan your time.

Avoid starting difficult assignments.

Surf the Web while working online.

BAD STUDY HABITS FROM LISTENING TWO	STRATEGIES FROM LISTENING ONE
MULTITASKING	
	Remove distractions, such as phones, games, Internet
PROCRASTINATION	
Waste time playing video games instead of studying	Set goals and put them in order of importance

Work in groups of three. Have a discussion about your study habits and strategies for improving them. Use information from the chart. In your discussion, you can ask these questions:

1. Do you multitask? If so, what do you do?

2. Do you procrastinate? Why or why not?

3. What strategies do you want to try?

4. What other strategies do you suggest for each other?

Example

A: Sam, do you multitask?

B: Yes, I do. I use my phone to text friends in class.

C: How about you, Justin?

GO TO MyEnglishLab TO CHECK WHAT YOU LEARNED.

3 FOCUS ON SPEAKING

VOCABULARY

REVIEW

Work with a partner. Complete the chart with the words and phrases from the box. Some words and phrases can be used in more than one column. Then think of two more words or phrases to add to each column. Take turns making sentences using a verb and word or phrase from the chart.

Example

A: I hope I can **achieve** my **goal** to become an engineer.

distractions	negative effects	a reward	tasks
goals	a positive attitude	strategies	time

ACHIEVE	AVOID	FOCUS ON	HAVE	MANAGE	PUT OFF	SET

1 🎧 Read and listen to the conversation.

A: Hey, how's it going?

B: Not bad. So what's up?

A: Oh, I'm on my way to the library. I need to **hit the books**. I've got a biology midterm tomorrow.

B: Biology? That should be easy.

A: Yeah, easy for you to say! You **aced** biology, right? My problem is I **cut class** a lot at the beginning of the semester, and I didn't study much because my roommate kept asking me to **hang out** with him. I really **fell behind**. Now I have to try to catch up on everything before tomorrow's test.

B: Ouch. Sounds like you really put it off to **the last minute**.

A: Tell me about it. I think I'm going to have to **pull an all-nighter** tonight.

B: I don't know. If you ask me, that's not such a good idea. I pulled a few all-nighters to study last semester, and I **bombed** the tests because I was too tired. It's just too hard to focus without enough sleep.

A: Yeah, well, I guess I'll learn the hard way. So, how about you? What are you up to?

B: I'm just on my way to my chemistry professor's office. There's a homework problem I can't **figure out**, and I need to get some help.

A: OK, well I'd better get to the library. I need to **cram** for that test!

B: Good luck!

2 Match the phrases on the left with the meanings on the right.

_____ **1.** hit the books

_____ **2.** ace

_____ **3.** cut class

_____ **4.** hang out

_____ **5.** fall behind

_____ **6.** the last minute

_____ **7.** pull an all-nighter

_____ **8.** bomb

_____ **9.** figure out

_____ **10.** cram

a. to stay up all night working on something

b. the last possible time that something can be done

c. to study

d. to understand or solve by thinking

e. to receive a grade of "A" or to complete something easily and successfully

f. to fail to do something as quickly as planned or as required

g. to quickly prepare right before a test

h. to skip a class or day of school without an excuse

i. to fail a test

j. to spend time in a certain place or with people

CREATE

Work with a partner. Choose one of the situations. Use at least 5–7 words from Review and Expand to write a conversation. Tell the class how many different words you used (but don't tell them which words). Perform your conversation for the class. The other students will listen and answer these questions:

- *Who are the speakers?*

- *What is the situation?*

- *Which speaker do you agree with? Why?*

- *Which vocabulary items did the speakers use? Did they use them correctly?*

Situation 1: You are roommates in college. Student A, you have a big test tomorrow and want to study. You're nervous. Student B, you want to have a party, but your roommate disagrees. You're upset with your roommate.

Situation 2: You are a student and a counselor. Student A, you need some help managing your time and learning better study habits. You ask the counselor for some help.

Situation 3: You are a student and a parent talking about school. Student A, you are not doing very well in school. Your parent wants you to explain why.

Situation 4: You are a student and a professor discussing an assignment that is due. Student A, you ask your professor for more time to finish the assignment. Your professor wants you to turn it in on time.

GRAMMAR

1 Read the questions and responses. Then answer the questions below.

Are you a student?	Yes, I am.
Is she in your class?	No, she isn't.
What is your major?	My major is English.
Do you procrastinate?	Yes, I do.
Does your class meet today?	No, it doesn't.
How often do you go to the library?	I go to the library every evening.
Where does your friend live?	He lives in the dormitory.
Why do they always eat out?	They don't know how to cook.

a. What is the verb in each question or answer? Which questions and answers have only one verb? Which ones have two verbs?

b. What form are the verbs?

SIMPLE PRESENT TENSE

1. Use the simple present tense to talk about actions that happen again and again, such as habits and routines.	I usually **go** to sleep at 11:00.
2. Use the simple present tense to tell facts.	About 20 percent of students **procrastinate** often.
3. Use the simple present with non-action verbs such as *be, have, know, understand, like, prefer, need,* and *want.*	I **prefer** to study alone.
4. In affirmative statements, use the base form of the verb, except for third person singular.	I **hope** to do better on the next test.
Add *–s* or *–es* with *he, she,* or *it.*	Ruben **likes** to play soccer after class.
5. In negative statements, use **does not** or **do not** before the base form of the verb. Use **doesn't** and **don't** in speaking and informal writing.	My math professor **doesn't allow** cell phones in class.
6. For questions in the simple present, use **do** or **does** before the subject	**Do** we **need** to finish this today? **Does** your family **call** you often?
7. Do not use **do** or **does** for questions with **be**.	**Is** she good at multitasking? What **are** your goals?

2 Work with a partner. Look at the conversation between a college counselor and a student. Complete the questions and answers with the correct forms of the verbs in parentheses. Use contractions when possible. Then, Student A, ask one of the questions. Student B, listen to the question and choose an answer and read it aloud. Switch roles after item 4. Finally, ask and answer the questions using your own information.

Questions

1. What _____ (be) your professional goals?

2. What _____ (be) your favorite class?

3. _____ your parents _____ (pressure) you to do well in school?

4. How often _____ you _____ (go) to the library?

5. _____ your roommate ever _____ (have) a negative effect on you?

6. When _____ you _____ (hang out) with friends?

7. _____ you _____ (get) enough sleep? You should get at least seven hours every night.

8. We _____ (not have) much time left today. _____ you _____ (have) any questions for me?

Answers

a. After class and on the weekends. We sometimes _____ (cook) dinner together or _____ (watch) a movie.

b. Yes, she _____ (do). She _____ (throw) a lot of parties. She _____ (make) a lot of noise, and she _____ (not clean) the apartment!

c. Not very often. I _____ (prefer) to study in my room.

d. No, not usually. I _____ (be) often really tired during the day because I _____ (stay up) late.

e. Yes, _____ you _____ (know) any good time management strategies?

f. I _____ (want) to become a lawyer. I _____ (think) I can do it.

g. Yes, sometimes they _____ (do). But I _____ (not listen) to them! It's too stressful.

h. It _____ (be) definitely my music class. My professor _____ (create) really interesting lessons.

■■■■■■■■■■■■■■■■■■■■■■■■■■■■■■ GO TO MyEnglishLab FOR MORE GRAMMAR PRACTICE.

PRONUNCIATION

1 🎧 Listen to the conversation. Notice the underlined syllables and words. How are they different from the other words?

A: Do you <u>have</u> any <u>home</u>work?

B: <u>Yeah</u>, I <u>do</u>. I <u>need</u> to <u>fin</u>ish my <u>Eng</u>lish <u>pa</u>per. It's <u>due</u> on <u>Mon</u>day. <u>How</u> about <u>you</u>?

A: <u>Well</u>, I'm in<u>vit</u>ed to a <u>par</u>ty on <u>Sat</u>urday. Do you <u>think</u> you can <u>come</u>?

B: <u>May</u>be. <u>Give</u> me a <u>call</u>!

STRESSED WORDS IN A SENTENCE

- In sentences, some words are *stressed* and others are *unstressed*. The stressed syllable is longer, higher, and louder than the other syllables in the sentence.

- Stressed words are usually *content words*. *Content words* are words that carry meaning in the sentence, such as nouns, main verbs, adjectives, and adverbs. In addition, we usually stress question words, and negatives, such as *not, isn't, aren't, don't, doesn't,* and *can't*.

- Stressed words are easier to hear. Putting stress on the content words helps listeners hear the important words in the sentence. This helps them pay attention to the meaning,

UNSTRESSED WORDS IN A SENTENCE

- Unstressed words are often *grammar words*:

  – helping verbs, such as *be* and *do,* and modal verbs, such as *can*

  – articles, such as *a, the,* and prepositions, such as *to, on, in, at, about*

  – pronouns, such as *I, you, he, she, it*

- Unstressed words are shorter, lower in pitch, and quieter than stressed words.

- Unstressed words are harder to hear. By not putting stress on unimportant words, we help listeners pay attention to the words in the sentence that carry the meaning.

- One way to make words weak when we are speaking is to use contractions, such as *I'm, it's, she's, he's, you're, we're, isn't, aren't, don't,* and *doesn't*

2 🎧 Listen to the conversation. Underline the stressed words in each sentence.

A: Hey, do you want to go to the beach? It's such a nice day.

B: Well, we don't have much time. Our class starts in two hours.

A: That isn't a problem. We can cut class today!

B: I'm not sure about that. I'd like to go to the beach, but I can't fall behind before the test.

A: OK. I'm not going to twist your arm[1]!

3 🎧 Listen again and check your answers. Then practice saying the conversation out loud with a partner.

---

[1] **twist your arm:** force you to do something

SPEAKING SKILL

EXPRESSING AGREEMENT AND DISAGREEMENT

1. In speaking, there are different phrases we can use to agree with others' opinions. Sometimes we want to express a strong agreement, and sometimes we want to express a weak agreement.

Expressing Agreement

I think that multitasking is a bad habit.

Strong

- I totally agree.
- I agree (with you/Sheila/Tom).
- I think so, too.
- I'm with you.
- That's true.
- Maybe
- I guess so

Weak

2. We can also disagree with others' opinions. Sometimes we want to express a strong disagreement, and sometimes we want to express a weak disagreement. In conversation, weak disagreements are more polite.

Expressing Disagreement

Strong

- I totally disagree.
- I disagree.
- I don't think so.
- Actually, I think . . .
- I'm not sure about that.
- I don't know.
- Maybe, but don't you think . . . ?

Weak

Work in a group. Read the following suggestions for school success. Take turns expressing your opinions about the statements. Do you think they are a good idea or a bad idea? Explain your opinions.

Example

A: I think it's a good idea to take classes early in the morning. Then you have more time during the day to do other things.

B: I don't know. I'm not a morning person, so I can't focus early in the morning.

C: I'm with you. I don't like waking up early.

1. Take classes early in the morning.

2. Find a study group for your difficult classes.

3. Never cram for tests.

4. Get at least seven hours of sleep every night.

5. Record your class lectures so you can listen again.

6. Use flash cards to help you remember information.

7. Visit a counselor to get advice.

8. Study in the library or another quiet place.

9. Limit your time texting or using social media.

10. Make a "to do" list every day.

11. Take naps between classes.

12. Exercise every day.

13. Join a club or sports team.

14. Talk to your family every day.

15. Don't hang out with friends on schooldays.

16. Avoid peer pressure[1] to make poor or unhealthy choices.

17. Keep a positive attitude. Tell yourself you can be successful!

---

[1] **peer pressure:** a strong feeling that you must do the same things as other people your age if you want them to like you

■■■■■■■■■■■■■■■■■ GO TO MyEnglishLab FOR MORE SKILL PRACTICE AND TO CHECK WHAT YOU LEARNED.

FINAL SPEAKING TASK

A survey is a list of questions that you ask other people to learn about their habits and opinions.

In this activity you will work in a group to survey your classmates about student life. Try to use the vocabulary, grammar, pronunciation, and language for expressing agreement and disagreement that you learned in the unit.*

Work in a group and follow the steps on the next page.

---

*For Alternative Speaking Topics, see page 47.

STEP 1: In your group, think of some questions you can ask to find out about your classmates' habits and opinions about school. Write your questions in the chart on the next page. Practice saying them with the correct pronunciation and stress.

Here are some ways you can begin your questions:

Do you . . . ? Example: Do you procrastinate?

Do you like to . . . ? Example: Do you like to exercise?

How often do you . . . ?

Where . . . ? When . . . ?

What do you think about . . . ?

How do you feel about . . . ?

Do you agree that . . . ?

QUESTIONS	NAME: _____	NAME: _____	NAME: _____
1.			
2.			
3.			
4.			

STEP 2: Go around the class and ask the other students your questions. Each person should speak to at least three different students in the class. Write each student's name in the chart. Write down their responses.

Example

A: Excuse me, can I ask you a few questions?
B: Sure.
A: How many hours do you study every day?
B: Hmmm . . . about three.
A: OK, thanks.

STEP 3: Share your results with your group. How many students agree with each other? How many disagree? Were there any surprising responses?

STEP 4: Report your results to the class. Each person should report the results of a different question. The other students should listen and take notes. What did you learn about your classmates?

UNIT PROJECT

Would you like to be a better student? Follow these steps to learn some strategies:

STEP 1: Work in small groups. Think of some challenges you have as a student. For example, maybe you have trouble remembering information for tests, or you need to manage your time better. Each of you should choose a different challenge you want to learn how to manage.

STEP 2: Now, work alone. Go to the library, look on the Internet, or interview someone who is an excellent student to learn about a strategy that can help you to deal with this challenge. Take notes. Your notes should include this information:

Student life challenge:

_____

Strategy or advice:

_____

How it works:

_____

Why it works:

_____

Do you want to try this strategy or advice? Why or why not?

_____

STEP 3: Report your information to the class.

Listening Task

Listen to your classmates' reports. Which strategy or piece of advice do you think is the most useful? Which is the most interesting?

ALTERNATIVE SPEAKING TOPICS

Discuss the following questions in a group. Explain your opinions.

1. Do you think it's better for students to live at home with their families, or away from home?

2. Do you prefer a large school or a small school? Why?

3. What do you think is the most important factor in student success?

4. Who do you ask for advice when you face challenges?

■■■■■■■■■■■■■■■■■■■■■■■■ GO TO MyEnglishLab TO DISCUSS ONE OF THE ALTERNATIVE TOPICS, WATCH A VIDEO ABOUT CREATIVITY, AND TAKE THE UNIT 2 ACHIEVEMENT TEST. ■■■■■■■■■■■■■■■

A PENNY SAVED IS A PENNY
Earned

1 FOCUS ON THE TOPIC

1. Look at the picture. This man wants the electronics but doesn't have enough money. What do you think he should do? Discuss with the class.

2. How do you usually pay for the things you need? For example, how often do you use cash, checks, credit cards, loans? What do you think is the best way to pay for things when you want to save money? Why do you think so?

3. Read the title of the unit. It is a famous American saying. What do you think it means?

GO TO MyEnglishLab TO CHECK WHAT YOU KNOW.

VOCABULARY

1 🎧 Read and listen to the timeline and the online article about the history of money and bartering.

MONEY SERIES

PART ONE: THE HISTORY OF MONEY AND BARTERING

9000 B.C.E.[1]	640 B.C.E.	806 C.E.[2]	1619
farm animals and plants used as money	first metal coins	first paper money made in China	tobacco used as money in Virginia

1762	1840	1950	1969	Today
first printed check used in England	first student loans made at Harvard University	first credit card	first ATM (Automatic Teller Machine)	electronic cash

[1] **B.C.E.** = Before the Common Era
[2] **C.E.** = the Common Era

Before people used money, they used other things that were **valuable** to them, such as plants or animals, to pay for things. Over the years, people developed more convenient ways to buy things such as loans, checks, and credit cards. Another convenient type of money is electronic money. Electronic money is used just like real money but can be saved on a computer or on an electronic cash card. Electronic money makes it easy to send money over the Internet. Today, there are many ways to buy things. But it is also easy to **spend** too much money. People can have problems when they spend more than they **earn**. As a result, many people are often looking for ways to save money.

One way for people to save money is bartering. Bartering means to exchange one thing for another without using money. For example, one person might **exchange** some food for some clothing or other **item** with **equal** value.

Before people used money, they bartered for the things they needed. Today, people, businesses, and governments still barter as a way to save money. For example, a business might barter for goods, such as machines, or **services**, such as **designing** a website, that another business can do for them. Some people use the Internet to find other people who **are interested in** bartering. Other people use community barter **networks**. A barter network is a group of people that trade with each other. A barter network **provides** its **members** with the chance to save money and get to know other people in their community.

---

2 Circle the best definition for each word or phrase in bold.

1. **valuable**
   - (a.) useful, important
   - b. living

2. **item**
   - a. a thing
   - b. clothing

3. **spend**
   - a. pay money
   - b. get money

4. **earn**
   - a. get money by working
   - b. pay money

5. **be interested in**
   - a. want or care about
   - b. understand

6. **exchange**
   - a. buy a new thing
   - b. trade; give one thing for another

7. **service**
   - a. something you do for someone
   - b. a thing you buy someone

8. **network**
   - a. group of people with the same interests
   - b. people in a community

9. **provides**
   - a. gives
   - b. gets

10. **member**
    - a. person who belongs to a group
    - b. person who barters

(continued on next page)

| 11. **designing** | **a.** creating | **b.** using |
| 12. **equal** | **a.** different | **b.** the same |

▪▪▪▪▪▪▪▪▪▪▪▪▪▪▪▪▪▪▪▪▪▪▪▪▪▪▪▪▪▪▪▪▪▪▪▪▪▪ *GO TO* MyEnglishLab *FOR MORE VOCABULARY PRACTICE.*

PREVIEW

Carol is speaking about the City Barter Network.

1 🎧 Listen to the beginning of *A Barter Network*. Then read each question and circle the correct answer.

1. What are you listening to?

   a. a radio announcement

   b. a meeting

   c. a class

2. Who is listening while Carol speaks?

   a. members of the barter network

   b. people who work for the barter network

   c. people who are interested in joining the network

2 Circle more than one answer to complete each sentence.

1. Carol is going to discuss . . .

   a. what bartering is.

   b. why people like to barter.

   c. how to use the barter network.

   d. how to join the network.

2. Carol will give information about . . .

   a. examples of things people barter

   b. how old the barter network is

   c. how many members belong to the network

   d. names of other members

   e. how to find other members

   f. an example of a barter exchange

MAIN IDEAS

1 🎧 Listen to the whole discussion about the City Barter Network. Look again at your predictions from the Preview section. Were any of your predictions correct? Did they help you understand the discussion?

2 Put a check (✓) next to the things that members do.

Members . . .

_____ barter for things and services.   _____ earn Time Dollars.

_____ only barter for services.   _____ use Time Dollars to buy services.

_____ need to provide a service before they can get one.   _____ spend money.

_____ earn money.

DETAILS

🎧 Listen to the barter network meeting again. Then read each statement. Write **T** *(true)* or **F** *(false)*. Correct the false statements.

_____ **1.** Members can list their services on a website.

_____ **2.** Most members provide services like cooking, cleaning, or fixing things.

_____ **3.** Members don't provide unusual services like taking photographs or giving music lessons.

_____ **4.** Some services are more valuable than others.

_____ **5.** Carol spent two hours cleaning another member's house.

_____ **6.** A member spent one hour fixing Carol's television.

_____ **7.** The man doesn't think he has skills.

_____ **8.** Carol needs someone to walk her dog.

■■■■■■■■■■■■■■■■■■■■■■■■■■■■■■■■■ GO TO MyEnglishLab *FOR MORE LISTENING PRACTICE.*

MAKE INFERENCES

UNDERSTANDING FEELINGS FROM INTONATION

An inference is a guess about something that is not directly stated. To make an inference, use information that you understand from what you hear. For example, listening for intonation can help you understand how a speaker is feeling. This can help you understand the speaker's meaning.

Different intonations express different feelings. A rising intonation can show you are surprised. A rising and falling intonation can show you are happy or interested, and a flat intonation can show that you are not interested.

🎧 Listen to the example. How does Woman 2 feel?

Example

WOMAN 1: But, ah . . . well, some people provide more unusual services like taking photographs, designing a website, or even giving music lessons.

WOMAN 2: Music lessons?! So, do you think I could get piano lessons? I've always wanted to learn how to play the piano.

WOMAN 1: Yeah, sure.

WOMAN 2: Wow! That's great!

In the example, the second woman's voice rises and falls. This shows she feels excited about learning to play the piano.

🎧 Listen to two excerpts from the meeting of the barter network. After listening to each excerpt, read the questions and circle the correct answers.

Excerpt One

1. How does the man feel about exchanging services?

   a. He feels excited.

   b. He doesn't feel excited.

2. How do you know?

   a. His voice is flat.

   b. His voice rises and falls.

1. How does the man feel about the woman's question?

    a. He's surprised.

    b. He isn't surprised.

2. How do you know?

    a. His voice is flat.

    b. His voice rises.

EXPRESS OPINIONS

Read the statements and circle *agree* or *disagree*. Then discuss your opinions in a group.

Example

A: I'd like to join a barter network because I like to save money. How about you?

B: I don't think so. It sounds like too much work to me.

1. I'd like to join a barter network.	agree	disagree
2. It's important to me to save money.	agree	disagree
3. Buying new things helps me feel good.	agree	disagree
4. I have services I can use to barter.	agree	disagree

■■■■■■■■■■■■■■■■■■■■■■■■■ *GO TO* MyEnglishLab *TO GIVE YOUR OPINION ABOUT ANOTHER QUESTION.*

VOCABULARY

Read the statements. Circle the best definition for the word or phrase in bold.

1. When I don't have something I need, I can always **borrow** it from my neighbor. It's easy to give it back when I am done.

   a. give to someone   **b.** get from someone temporarily

2. My house is very crowded and full of **stuff** I don't need. I should clean it out.

   a. things, items   **b.** full

3. Some things are **necessities**. An example is food because you can't live without it.

   a. things you like to have   **b.** things you must have

4. I like new clothes, but to save money, sometimes I buy **used** clothes. They are cheaper.

   a. new   **b.** not new

5. **I bet** you would like the new computer I bought. It's really fast!

   a. I think I know   **b.** I am not sure if something is true

6. I only bought two things today—groceries and gas for my car. **That's it**!

   a. That's what I bought.   **b.** That's all

■■■■■■■■■■■■■■■■■■■■■■■■■■■ GO TO MyEnglishLab *FOR MORE VOCABULARY PRACTICE.*

COMPREHENSION

Listen to the conversation between two members of the City Barter Network. Circle the best answer to complete each statement.

1. The Compact is a group of people who promised _____.

   a. to barter for a year

   b. not to buy anything new for a year

2. Members of the Compact can buy new _____.

   a. food, medicine, and necessities

   b. food, cars, and necessities

Used items in a thrift store

3. The members of the Compact think _____.

   a. clothes, cars, and electronics are too expensive

   b. most people have too much stuff they don't need

4. Members of the Compact _____ to get what they need.

   a. borrow, buy things used, or barter

   b. buy used things and barter for food

5. Mark needed to buy _____.

   a. new paint

   b. a new house

6. There are _____ of members in the Compact.

   a. hundreds

   b. thousands

7. Natalie likes shopping for _____.

   a. used clothes

   b. new clothes

LISTENING SKILL

EMPHATIC STRESS

Emphatic stress means putting extra stress, or emphasis, on certain words in a phrase or sentence. We *emphasize* a word or words that are especially important for understanding the speaker's meaning. When we emphasize a word, the stressed syllable is higher, longer, and louder than a syllable with regular stress.

Example

🎧 Read and listen to the conversation.

WOMAN: No Kidding! You aren't going to buy ANYTHING new for a whole YEAR?

MAN: Well . . . actually, we CAN buy new necessities, things, you know, that you NEED . . .

The woman says, "You aren't going to buy ANYTHING new for a whole YEAR?" She can't believe people really don't buy anything at all for such a long time, so she stresses the words *anything* and *year*.

The man responds that they CAN buy things they NEED. In this sentence, the man wants to bring attention to the fact that in the Compact, people can buy some necessities, or things they need. He emphasizes the words *can* and *need*.

🎧 Listen to the excerpts. What words are the speakers emphasizing? Discuss why with a partner.

Excerpt One

What words does the man emphasize? _____

What words does the woman emphasize? _____

Why do they emphasize those words? _____

Excerpt Two

What word does the man emphasize? _____

Why do you think he emphasizes that word? _____

■ *GO TO* MyEnglishLab *FOR MORE SKILL PRACTICE.*

STEP 1: Organize

1 Look at the list of goods (things you can buy) and services (things you pay people to do for you) mentioned in the listenings. Write each item in the correct column in the chart.

car	computer	medicine
~~clean someone's house~~	fix a television	paint someone's house
clothes	food	walk someone's dog
	give someone piano lessons	

GOODS	SERVICES
	clean someone's house

2 How can members of the Compact get the goods and services they need? Write each good and service from the chart on page 59 in the correct place on the graphic organizer. Then compare your answers with a classmate's.

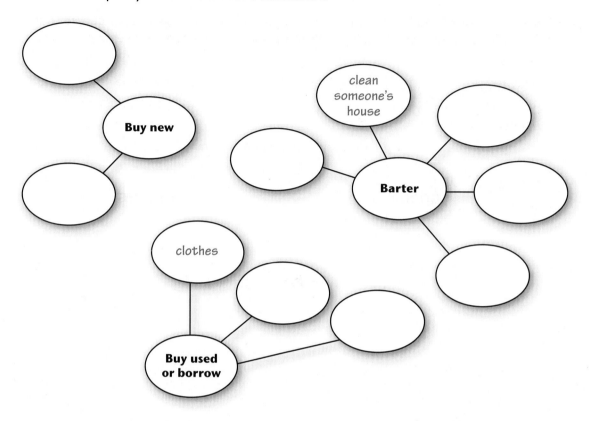

STEP 2: Synthesize

Work with a partner. Imagine you are in the City Barter Network and the Compact. Student A, say what you need. Student B, suggest a way to get each thing. Use the information from Step 1.

Example

A: I want someone to clean my house.

B: You can get that by bartering.

GO TO MyEnglishLab *TO CHECK WHAT YOU LEARNED.*

3 FOCUS ON SPEAKING

VOCABULARY

Complete the conversations with words from the box. Use the underlined words to help you. Then work with a partner to practice reading the conversations aloud. Switch roles after item 4.

be interested in	I bet	stuff
borrow	necessities	That's it
equal	services	~~used~~
exchange	spend	valuable

1. **A:** I bought a chair at a thrift store yesterday. <u>It isn't new</u>, but it's very nice.

   B: Do you really like to buy _____*used*_____ things?

2. **A:** This sweater is too big. I need to take it back to the store and <u>trade</u> it for a smaller one.

   B: Does that store let you _____ things?

3. **A:** Do you want to go shopping? I need to get some <u>things</u> for my apartment.

   B: No, thanks. I already have too much _____.

4. **A:** I wish I knew how to do something <u>useful</u>, like fixing cars.

   B: Yeah, you're right. Fixing cars is a _____ skill.

5. **A:** I <u>need</u> to buy a new MP3 player and download some new songs.

   B: Really? Are an MP3 player and new music really _____?

6. **A:** I don't want to <u>pay</u> a lot of money for a television.

   B: How much do you want to _____?

7. **A:** That department store <u>does so many things</u> for you. They even have personal shoppers, people who help you choose what to buy.

   B: Yeah, they do offer a lot of _____.

(continued on next page)

8. A: Do you think these two cameras are <u>the same</u>?

   B: Yeah, I think they are pretty _____.

9. A: My car broke down. Can I <u>use yours</u> to get to school today?

   B: Sure, you can _____ it anytime.

10. A: I am thinking about taking a class. I <u>want to</u> learn more about saving money.

   B: That's sounds good. Maybe I will join you. I _____ that as well.

11. A: You mentioned that new movie. I <u>think I know</u> what you want to do tonight!

   B: _____ you do!

12. A: We need some milk and eggs from the store.

   B: _____. We really don't need much.

EXPAND

1 🎧 Read and listen to the newsletter article about Freecycle.

THE BARTER NETWORK NEWSLETTER
By Carol Meyer

This Week's Money-Saving Tip: Freecycle®

1 Last week I wrote about thrift stores, where you can get a good price on used items and save lots of money. But an even better way to save money is *Freecycle*. *Freecycle* is an online group. People give away things they don't need anymore—for free! Other people get things they need, for free, so they don't have to **pay an arm and a leg**.

2 When you join *Freecycle*, you select a group that is near you. There are groups all over the world, in 85 countries, so there is probably a group near you. After you join, you can see lists of items that people are giving away near your home.

3 People list all kinds of things: furniture, clothes, artwork, electronics, and more. You may need something that you can't **afford** to buy. But on *Freecycle*, it's free! What a great **bargain**!

4   Another way to save money is to go to flea markets where people sell stuff cheap. Some people like **to bargain** with the sellers. I got **a good deal** last weekend at a flea market on a jacket. At first, the seller asked $100 for it, but I bargained with him until he agreed to take only $50. But my friend got an even better deal. She used *Freecycle* and got a jacket for free; no **cost**. And the jacket was **worth** a lot of money!

5   At *Freecycle* or at a flea market you may have to spend some extra time looking for what you want, but it can be a lot of fun. You can also save a lot of money. It's really **worth it!**

2 Match the phrases on the left with the definitions on the right.

_____ **1.** to pay an arm and a leg   **a.** to have a particular value

_____ **2.** to afford   **b.** to have a particular price

_____ **3.** a bargain   **c.** to have enough money to pay for something

_____ **4.** to bargain   **d.** to get a good price on something

_____ **5.** to get a good deal   **e.** to spend a lot of money

_____ **6.** to cost   **f.** to discuss the price of something you are buying

_____ **7.** to be worth   **g.** to be good to do even though you made an effort

_____ **8.** to be worth it   **h.** something you buy for less than the usual price

CREATE

Work in a small group. Take turns asking and answering the questions. Use the boldfaced words and vocabulary from Review and Expand in your answers.

1. Do you like **to bargain** with sellers when you shop? Do you bargain when you buy from street vendors? Why or why not?

2. Do you like to buy things **used**? Why or why not? If yes, what are some things that you like to buy used? What are some things you never buy used?

3. Name a store or place to shop that you think has good **bargains**. What kinds of bargains can you get there?

4. Name something you bought that you **got a good deal** on. Where did you get it? Why do you think it was a good deal?

5. Do you have a lot of **stuff** in your house? What do you usually do with stuff that you don't use anymore—do you prefer to keep it, throw it away, or give it to someone else?

(continued on next page)

A Penny Saved Is a Penny Earned   63

6. Name something you own that was **cheap** to buy. How much did it cost? Name something that you **paid an arm and a leg** for.

7. Do you own something that is **worth** more now than when you bought it? How much did you **spend** on it? Was it **worth it**?

GO TO MyEnglishLab FOR MORE VOCABULARY PRACTICE.

GRAMMAR

1 Read the sentences. Look at the underlined words. Then answer the questions below.

I need to find a <u>cheaper</u> place to shop.

The department store is <u>bigger</u> than the thrift store.

a. What is the adjective in the first sentence? What does it describe? What two letters does the adjective end with?

b. What is the adjective in the second sentence? What does it describe? What word comes after *bigger*?

COMPARATIVE ADJECTIVES	
1. Use the comparative form of the adjective to compare two people, places, or things. Use *than* before the second person, place, or thing.	This car is **cheaper** *than* that one.
2. Add *–er* to form the comparative of short (one-syllable) adjectives. Add *–r* if the adjective ends in *e*.	cheap cheap**er** old old**er** close close**r**
3. When a one-syllable adjective ends in a consonant + vowel + consonant, double the last consonant and add *–er*.	big big**ger** hot hot**ter**
4. When two-syllable adjectives end in *–y*, change the *y* to *i* and add *–er*	easy eas**ier** funny funn**ier**
5. Some adjectives have irregular comparative forms.	good **better** bad **worse**
6. To form the comparative of most adjectives of two or more syllables, add *more* before the adjective. *Less* is the opposite of *more*.	No service is *more* **valuable** than another one. Used clothing is *less* **expensive** than new clothing.

Introducing the new
INDULGE

Buy a new
Indulge
and drive in comfort,
style, and safety for only $50,000!

This week's special: a used
Pee Wee

This Pee Wee
is almost new, and it
runs great! It gets excellent
gas mileage, and it's on sale now for only $4,000!

2 Work with a partner. Look at the ads for the cars. Take turns making sentences comparing the two cars. Use the adjectives from the box. Then say which car you would like to buy and why.

bad for the environment	easy to park	nice
big	expensive	old
cheap to drive	good for a big family	safe
comfortable		

Example

A: The Indulge is bigger than the Pee Wee.

B: The Indulge is more expensive than the Pee Wee.

3 Work with a partner. Student A, you want to buy the Indulge. Student B, you want to buy the Pee Wee. Take turns making sentences comparing the two cars. Use adjectives from the box or other adjectives you can think of.

Example

A: I want to buy the Indulge because it's bigger than the Pee-Wee.

B: Yeah, but the Pee-Wee is cheaper to drive.

■■■■■■■■■■■■■■■■■■■■■■■■■■■■■■■■■ *GO TO* MyEnglishLab *FOR MORE GRAMMAR PRACTICE.*

PRONUNCIATION

NUMBERS AND PRICES

When we say the numbers 13 through 19, -*teen* is stressed and the letter **t** in -*teen* sounds like /t/. When we say the numbers 20, 30, 40, 50, 60, 70, 80, and 90, the first syllable is stressed and the letter **t** in -*ty* sounds like a "fast" /d/.

🎧 Listen to the examples.

Example 1

13	16	19
/thirteen/	/sixteen/	/nineteen/
30	60	90
/thirdy/	/sixdy/	/ninedy/

There are two ways to say prices.

🎧 Listen to the examples. Pay attention to what is stressed.

Example 2

$4.29
four dollars and twenty-nine cents
four twenty-nine

$53.99
fifty-three dollars and ninety-nine cents
fifty-three ninety-nine

1 🎧 Listen to the numbers. Circle the number you hear.

1. 13   30

2. 14   40

3. 15   50

4. 16   60

5. 17   70

6. 18   80

7. 19   90

2 Work with a partner. Look at the numbers in Exercise 1. Take turns. Say a number. Remember to stress the correct syllable. Your partner points to the number you say.

3 🎧 Listen and write the prices you hear. Then practice saying them aloud in two different ways.

1. $_____

2. $_____

3. $_____

4. $_____

5. $_____

4 Work with a partner. Take turns asking each other how much you usually spend on the items listed. Write your partner's answers. Share the information with your classmates.

Example

A: How much do you usually spend on a haircut?

B: I spend thirty dollars. How about you?

A: I spend fifteen dollars.

1. a haircut $_____

2. a movie ticket $_____

3. your phone bill $_____

4. a meal in a restaurant $_____

SPEAKING SKILL

NEGOTIATING—MAKING SUGGESTIONS AND COMING TO AN AGREEMENT

When two or more people need to make a decision together, they need to negotiate; they need to come to an agreement. When negotiating, you need to make suggestions until each person agrees.

MAKING SUGGESTIONS	AGREEING WITH SUGGESTIONS	DISAGREEING WITH SUGGESTIONS
Let's buy this chair.	OK. / All right.	Well, I don't know. How about . . . ?
Why don't we go to the thrift store?	That's fine with me.	I have another idea. Why don't we . . . ?
How about buying a used car instead of a new one?	That's a good idea.	I don't think so.
Would you like to sell your computer?	Let's do it.	
	It's a deal.	
	OK. Why not?	

1 Look at the list of things. Pretend you have **$2,500** to buy things for your new house or apartment. Make a list of the things you would like to get.

used couch—$100   plants—$50

new couch—$650   pet kitten—$75

large armchair—$300   pet dog—$130

large floor rug—$200   computer—$800

lamp—$25   stereo speakers—$250

bookcase—$115   used piano—$300

painting—$175   small used television—$85

video game player—$200   large new television—$700

Your List

_____   _____   _____

_____   _____   _____

2 Now work in a small group. Take turns suggesting things to buy. When everyone agrees, write your group's list below.

Example

A: Let's buy the used couch for $100.

B: Well, I don't know. I don't want a used couch. How about buying the new one?

C: But it costs a lot. Why don't we buy the chair?

Your Group's List

_____   _____   _____

_____   _____   _____

3 Share your group's list with another group. Explain why your group chose each thing. The other group listens and answers. Did you choose the same things? Why or why not?

■■■■■■■■■■■■■■■■■ GO TO MyEnglishLab FOR MORE SKILL PRACTICE AND TO CHECK WHAT YOU LEARNED.

FINAL SPEAKING TASK

In this activity, you will practice bartering for goods and services with your classmates. Try to use the vocabulary, grammar, pronunciation, and language for negotiating that you learned in the unit.*

Follow the steps.

STEP 1: Get five blank cards. On four of the cards write the following:

a. name of an item you would like to exchange (and a drawing, if you'd like)

b. how old it is

c. how much money you think it is worth now

Do this for four items. On the fifth card, write a service you can provide, such as cook dinner.

_____

*For Alternative Speaking Topics, see page 71.

A Penny Saved Is a Penny Earned   69

STEP 2: Go around the class and barter with your classmates. Compare your items and services and negotiate with each other until you come to an agreement. When you come to an agreement, trade your cards.

Example

A: How about exchanging your television for my computer?

B: But my television is newer than your computer.

A: Yeah, but my computer is more valuable.

B: Thanks, but that's not worth it. I want to keep looking.

OR

B: OK. It's a deal.

STEP 3: Report your exchanges to the class.

Example

A: I traded a two-year-old television worth $300 for a three-year-old computer worth $350.

B: That's a pretty good deal.

C: Well, I paid an arm and a leg for a TV.

Listening Task

Listen to your classmates' reports. Who made the most exchanges? Who got the best deal?

UNIT PROJECT

Before you buy something, especially something expensive, it's a good idea to do comparison shopping. When you comparison shop, you compare the different choices and then decide which is the best one to buy.

STEP 1: Think of something you would like to buy, such as a camera, a cell phone or other electronic device, or a jacket. Then go to a store or use the Internet to compare two different kinds. Compare the item and price. You may want to read some reviews to see what other people think of it. Answer the questions about your choice. If the question doesn't apply, write N/A (not applicable). Take notes and write the information in the chart below.

	ITEM 1	ITEM 2
HOW MUCH DOES IT COST?		
WHAT DOES IT LOOK LIKE?		
WHAT CAN IT DO?		
HOW WELL IS IT MADE?		
HOW BIG IS IT?		
DO YOU WANT TO BUY IT?		
WHY OR WHY NOT?		

STEP 2: Report back to the class, telling which item you would like to buy and why.

Listening Task

Listen to your classmates' reports. Do you agree with their choices? Which item would you like to buy? Discuss your opinions with a partner.

ALTERNATIVE SPEAKING TOPICS

Work in a small group. Discuss the questions.

1. Do you think that most people have too much stuff? Why or why not? Give examples.

2. Do you think the Compact is a good idea or a bad idea? Why? Could you keep a promise not to buy anything new for a year? Explain.

3. Do people in your culture buy and sell used stuff? If yes, where? If no, why not?

4. What kinds of things do you only want to buy new? What will you buy used? Why will you buy some things used but others new?

GO TO MyEnglishLab TO DISCUSS ONE OF THE ALTERNATIVE TOPICS, WATCH A VIDEO ABOUT MONEY, AND TAKE THE UNIT 3 ACHIEVEMENT TEST.

WHAT HAPPENED TO Etiquette?

1 FOCUS ON THE TOPIC

1. Look at the photo. What is happening?

2. In your opinion, is this polite or not? Why do you think so?

3. *Etiquette* means the rules we follow to behave (act) politely. What are some other actions that you think are polite? What are some that are rude (not polite)? Why do you think they are rude? Discuss your opinions with the class.

GO TO MyEnglishLab TO CHECK WHAT YOU KNOW.

2 FOCUS ON LISTENING

VOCABULARY

1 🎧 Read and listen to the beginning of a radio show.

> **HOST:** Thanks for tuning into *Your World*. In today's show, we're going to focus on **manners**.
>
> Maybe, like me, you were **raised** by your parents to be **courteous**. My mother always said, "**Treat** others as you want them to treat you." In other words, show **respect** to others. Many cultures have the same idea. In English, this is called "the golden rule."
>
> But what is considered to be polite **behavior** will be different depending on your culture. For example, in some countries, when you're invited to dinner at someone's home, you should arrive on time. If not, it's considered rude. But in other countries, when you're invited to someone's home for dinner, it's rude to arrive *on time*. You should instead arrive 30 minutes late! So, what's polite depends on where you are.
>
> But behavior can be different even in the same culture. For example, imagine you are at work and have a file of important **documents** to give to your boss. On your way to her office, you drop the whole file! Will someone stop to help you pick them up? Maybe. Maybe not. We all **appreciate** it when others are polite to us, but it seems like many people just aren't polite anymore.
>
> In a recent survey[1] that was **conducted** in the U.S., 76 percent of the people said that manners are changing and people are less courteous now than they were in the past. They believe that these days, Americans are more **likely** to behave and speak in a rude way than they have in the past. Is this true? Are people becoming less courteous? Let's find out.

---

[1] **survey:** a set of questions you ask a large number of people to learn their opinions or behavior

2 Match the words on the left with the definitions on the right.

___b___ 1. manners

_____ 2. to be raised

_____ 3. courteous

_____ 4. treat

_____ 5. respect

_____ 6. appreciate

_____ 7. behavior

_____ 8. conduct (v)

_____ 9. document

_____ 10. likely

a. used to show the chance that something will happen

b. ~~polite ways to behave or speak~~

c. be taken care of as a child: be brought up

d. to act or think toward someone in a particular way

e. a piece of paper with official information on it

f. polite

g. feel or show care for or attention to something

h. to be grateful or thankful (for something)

i. the way someone acts

j. to plan and do something, such as a test or study

■■■■■■■■■■■■■■■■■■■■■■■■■■■■■■■■■ GO TO MyEnglishLab FOR MORE VOCABULARY PRACTICE.

PREVIEW

Many people think the general public doesn't have good manners anymore. Discuss this idea with a partner. Then, listen to the radio show.

🎧 Listen to the beginning of the radio show called *What Ever Happened to Manners?* How do you think Sarah Jones did an international study of manners? List three possible ways.

1. _____

2. _____

3. _____

MAIN IDEAS

1. 🎧 Listen to the complete interview. Look at your predictions from the Preview section. Were any of your predictions correct? Did your predictions help you understand the interview?

2. Circle the correct answer to each question.

1. How did the reporters conduct their study?

   a. They asked people for their opinions about manners.

   b. They observed people's language and behavior.

   c. They gave people a written test of polite behaviors.

2. Where did the reporters conduct their study?

   a. in different coffee shops

   b. in different workplaces

   c. in different cities

3. What behaviors were included in the study?

   a. holding the door for someone, helping someone pick up some documents, and letting someone sit down

   b. helping someone pick up some documents, helping someone cross the street, and saying "thank you"

   c. holding the door for someone, helping someone pick up some documents, and saying "thank you"

4. What reason did most people give for being courteous?

    a. They were raised to be courteous.

    b. They want to help others.

    c. They follow "the golden rule."

5. Who did the reporters test?

    a. all kinds of people

    b. students and businesspeople

    c. only cashiers

DETAILS

Listen to the interview again. Then complete the summary of the survey.

Two reporters went to large cities all around the world. They went to _____
                                                    1.

countries. The reporters did three tests: a _____ test, a _____
                                                2.   3.

drop, and a customer _____ test.
                                     4.

For the door test, they wanted to see if people would _____
                                                        5.

_____ _____ for the reporters. For the second test, they

wanted to see if anyone would help them pick up a _____ of important
                                                              6.

papers. For the customer service test, they wanted to see if people who work in stores were

polite and said _____ _____.
                                7.

In the most courteous city, _____ percent of the people passed the door test,
                                         8.

but when the reporters dropped their papers, only _____ percent helped
                                                 9.

pick them up. For the customer service test, _____ out of 20 cashiers passed
                                                  10.

the test. Men were more _____ to help than women. In the document test,
                                 11.

(continued on next page)

What Happened to Etiquette?   **77**

_____ percent of the men and _____ percent of the women

12.   13.

helped the reporters. In the study, _____ _____ was the most

14.

courteous city.

GO TO MyEnglishLab FOR MORE LISTENING PRACTICE.

MAKE INFERENCES

UNDERSTANDING CONTRASTING IDEAS

An inference is a guess about something that is not directly stated. To make an inference, use information that you understand from what you hear.

We *contrast* two different ideas when we want to show how they are different. To help us understand contrasts, speakers put extra stress on the words in the sentence that show how two ideas are different. This helps listeners to focus on the key words that will help them to understand the contrasting ideas.

⌒ Listen to the example. Which words does the speaker stress? What are the two ideas the speaker is contrasting?

Example

   You know, what I'm curious about is why *some* people *are* courteous and some *others aren't*.

In this example, the speaker stresses the words *some* and *are*, and also the words *others* and *aren't*. The speaker is contrasting two ideas: *some people are courteous, but other people are not.*

⌒ Listen to two excerpts from the interview. After listening to each excerpt, write down two pairs of words or numbers that are stressed. What are the two ideas the speaker is contrasting?

Excerpt One

Stressed words: _almost everyone_   _door_

_____   _____

Contrasting ideas: 1. _Almost everyone held the door._

2. _____

Excerpt Two

Stressed words: _____   _____

_____   _____

Contrasting ideas: 1. _____

2. _____

EXPRESS OPINIONS

Discuss the questions with the class.

1. In your opinion, are people less polite these days than in the past? Give examples to explain your opinion.

2. Where did you learn manners: At home? At school? At a religious institution?

3. New York City scored as the number one city for good manners. Are you surprised? Why or why not?

4. How do you think people in your hometown would do on Sarah's manners test? Do you think they would pass? Why or why not?

■■■■■■■■■■■■■■■■■■■■■■■■■■■ *GO TO* MyEnglishLab *TO GIVE YOUR OPINION ABOUT ANOTHER QUESTION.*

LISTENING TWO OUR LISTENERS RESPOND—WHY IS THERE A LACK OF MANNERS?

VOCABULARY

🎧 Listen to the following words. Then read the sentences and choose the best definition for each word. Circle your answers.

confusing	face-to-face	text
electronic device	immediate response	

1. Etiquette can be **confusing** when you travel to a new culture. The rules of politeness may be different, and you may not know how to behave politely.

   a. difficult to understand

   b. difficult to say

2. Cell phones are a type of **electronic device** that helps us to communicate with each other faster.

   a. a machine that is fast

   b. electronic equipment used to achieve a purpose

(continued on next page)

3. I think it's more polite to say you are sorry to someone **face-to-face**, instead of by email.

    a. online

    b. in person

4. I sent a text message to my friend Karl 10 minutes ago inviting him to my party, and he sent an **immediate response** saying he can come.

    a. a polite answer

    b. a fast answer

5. You should never **text** when you are driving. It's not safe to use your phone and drive at the same time.

    a. send a written message by phone

    b. send an email through your computer

GO TO MyEnglishLab FOR MORE VOCABULARY PRACTICE.

COMPREHENSION

🎧 Listen to the second part of the radio show. Listeners were invited to call in with their ideas on why people are rude. Look at the list of reasons. Check (✓) the reasons you hear.

There is a lack[1] of manners because . . .

_____ parents don't spend enough time teaching their kids manners.

_____ people don't know each other well, so they are less polite.

_____ children don't learn manners at school anymore.

_____ living with people from many different cultures is confusing.

_____ of electronic devices, people give immediate short responses.

_____ people follow the behavior they see on TV.

_____ people forget how to talk to someone face-to-face.

---

[1] **lack:** not having any or enough of something

LISTENING SKILL

UNDERSTANDING SUMMARIES

In *summaries*, speakers repeat the main points of what was said. When they *summarize*, speakers include only the most important information, and they leave out details. Listening for summary sentences can help you to understand and remember the main ideas of a listening.

Example

🎧 Listen to the example:

Host: Well, we're out of time, but to wrap up: we need more family time, a better understanding of our different cultures, and more face-to-face time . . . certainly some things to think about! That's all for now, until next week.

In the example, the host summarized all of the caller's comments in one sentence: *We need good manners at home, a better understanding of our different cultures, and more face-to-face time.*

🎧 Listen to the following excerpts from *Our Listeners Respond—Why Is There a Lack of Manners?* Take notes of the key words. Then write a sentence that summarizes the main point(s) of what the speaker said. Then listen to how the host summarizes the callers' opinions. Compare your sentences. Did you include the same information?

Excerpt One

Key words: _____

My summary sentence: _____

The host's summary sentence: _____

Excerpt Two

Key words: _____

My summary sentence: _____

The host's summary sentence: _____

■ *GO TO* MyEnglishLab *FOR MORE SKILL PRACTICE.*

STEP 1: Organize

Complete the chart. Look at the list of ideas from Listenings One and Two. Each idea belongs to one of the categories in the chart below. Categorize each idea and write it in the correct column. Then compare your completed chart with a partner's.

~~Small things like holding the door are easy to do.~~

~~Parents don't teach manners at home.~~

People communicate using electronic devices, such as cell phones.

You don't know how long to hold the door for someone.

Sometimes your hands are full and you can't help.

It shows respect for others.

People follow "the golden rule."

People from other cultures may seem rude but they have different rules of etiquette.

People are raised to be polite.

REASONS FOR COURTEOUS BEHAVIOR	REASONS FOR IMPOLITE BEHAVIOR
• *Small things like holding the door are easy to do.*	• *Parents don't teach manners at home.*
•	•
•	•
•	•
	•

STEP 2: Synthesize

Work with a partner. Student A, you are a reporter interviewing people on the street about manners. Ask questions. Student B, answer Student A's questions. Use the information from Step 1. Then switch roles and repeat the conversation.

Example

A: Hello. I'm interviewing people about manners. Can you give me an example of courteous behavior?

B: Sure. I think it's polite to hold the door for someone.

A: True. Why do you think people do that?

B: Well, you're opening the door anyway. It's an easy thing to do.

A: But some people aren't courteous. Why is that?

B: I think one reason is parents don't spend enough time teaching their children manners anymore.

GO TO MyEnglishLab TO CHECK WHAT YOU LEARNED.

VOCABULARY

REVIEW

Read the magazine column about etiquette. Write the correct word in the blank. Use the words from the box.

appreciate	confusing	face-to-face	respect	treat
behavior	courteous	raised	rude	

Ask Miss Manners

Dear Miss Manners,

Thanks for all your great advice. I really _____ it. I wish everyone cared
1.
about manners. I think people are not as polite now as they used to be. It seems that every day someone gets in front of me in line or starts texting when I'm talking to them. People are just not _____.
2.

—Clara

Dear Clara,

Unfortunately, there does seem to be a lack of manners these days. The question is, what do we do about it? I think the important thing to remember is to _____ others in a nice way.
3.
If we can all just remember to _____
4.
each other, I think we can all get along.

(continued on next page)

Dear Miss Manners,

I'm really bothered by children who misbehave in public places. I know children are all _____ differently, so you see a lot
5.
of different _____, but I want to
6.
do something about it.

I was shopping the other day, and some kids were running around. It was hard to shop. What should I do in that situation?

—Annoyed Shopper

Dear Annoyed Shopper,

Well, one idea is to tell the manager. It's really the manager's job to deal with customers. It's not always best for you to talk to the person

_____.
7.

Dear Miss Manners,

Sometimes I feel people from other countries are being _____ because they
8.
talk so loud. What do you suggest I do?

—Julius K.

Dear Julius K.,

Nowadays, we live with people from all over the world. We don't always speak the same language or have the same rules of etiquette. I know it can be _____, when we don't understand
9.
another person's culture. But we all have to learn to get along.

EXPAND

1 ⊙ Read and listen to the conversation. Then take turns reading the conversation with a partner.

A: I had a terrible day today.

B: Really? What happened?

A: Well, do you remember that girl from my math class that I was telling you about?

B: Yeah . . .

A: Well, I finally got up the courage and asked her to **go out** with me.

B: So what did she say?

A: That's the problem. I asked her out two weeks ago, and she didn't respond at all until yesterday.

B: Oh no. Why did she **leave you hanging** for so long?

A: I don't know, but she finally agreed to go see a movie with me tonight. I was so excited. I was really **looking forward to** it.

B: So, what happened?

A: Well, I waited at the movie theater for almost half an hour. Finally, she texted me to **call off** our date. She gave me an excuse saying she needed to study for a test.

B: Oh, that's too bad. It was really rude of her to **blow** you **off** like that. I hate to say this, but it sounds like she never wanted to go out with you in the first place. Maybe she was afraid to **turn** you **down** because she didn't want to hurt your feelings.

A: Yeah, you're probably right. What a **bummer**.

B: Cheer up! She doesn't sound worth it. And hey, what time is the next show? Maybe we could still catch that movie!

A: Thanks, but I think **I'll have to pass**. I don't feel like doing anything now. Can I **take a rain check**?

B: Sure, no problem. Maybe next weekend.

A: OK, let's do that.

2 Match the phrase on the left with its meaning on the right.

_____ **1.** go out

_____ **2.** leave someone hanging

_____ **3.** look forward to

_____ **4.** call something off

_____ **5.** blow off

_____ **6.** turn down

_____ **7.** bummer

_____ **8.** I'll have to pass

_____ **9.** take a rain check

a. to cancel or delay an event; to decide that an event will not happen

b. a situation that is bad, annoying, or disappointing

c. to tell someone that you can't do something with them now, but you would like to do it at another time

d. I can't accept your invitation.

e. to ignore someone

f. to say "no" to an invitation

g. go on a date; to have a romantic relationship

h. to be excited and pleased about something that is going to happen

i. to keep someone waiting for a decision or answer

Work in groups of four. You will have a debate about each of the actions listed below. For each action, each student will take a side—either you think it is courteous or rude. Use the words from Review and Expand in the box.

appreciate	confusing	leave someone hanging	take a rain check
behavior	courteous	look forward to	treat
blow off	face-to-face	raised	turn down
bummer	go out	respect	
call something off	I'll have to pass	rude	

Actions

Taking your shoes off before entering someone's home

Talking on your cell phone while in a restaurant with friends

Not responding to an invitation

Texting while having a conversation with someone

Throwing garbage on the ground (littering)

Example

A: I think taking your shoes off before entering someone's house is very *courteous*. It shows *respect* for the other person. I really *appreciate* it when people take their shoes off when they come to my house. Plus, it helps to keep my house clean.

B: Really? I don't think it's courteous to take them off. I wasn't *raised* to do that, so I don't think it shows *a lack of manners* to leave them on.

GO TO MyEnglishLab FOR MORE VOCABULARY PRACTICE.

GRAMMAR

1 Read the examples. Then answer the questions.

Can you hand me that pencil?

Could you please hold the door open for me?

Would you help me pick up my papers?

Could you help me, please?

a. What is the first word in each question? What answer do you expect?

b. Look at the main verb in each question. What is the form?

CAN, COULD AND WOULD IN POLITE REQUESTS	
1. Use *can*, *could* and *would* when you want to make a polite request or politely ask someone for something. *Could* and *would* have the same meaning. *Could* and *would* are modals. Modals are verbs that are usually used with other verbs to express certain ideas. The verb that follows *could* and *would* is in the simple form.	**Can** you do me favor? **Could** you **hold** the door for me? **Would** you **help** me with the dishes?
2. When your request contains another question, use statement word order in the second question.	Could you tell me **where the restroom is**?
3. *Please* is often used to make the question even more polite.	Could you **please** hold the door for me? Would you help me with the dishes, **please**?
4. To answer politely, use these typical responses. When we say *no*, it's polite to give a reason.	Yes, of course. Certainly. I'd be glad to. I'd be happy to. Sure. No problem. Sorry, I can't. I have to go to class now. I'd like to, but I'm busy.

2 Work with a partner. Student A, use the situations below to make a polite request. Student B, respond politely. Then switch roles.

Example:

A: Could you please hold the door for me?

B: Sure, no problem.

1. Hold the door for me.
2. Help me pick up these papers.
3. Turn off your cell phone.
4. Tell me the time.
5. Tell me what time your store closes.
6. Lend me your phone.
7. Help me move this weekend.
8. Show me how to do this assignment.
9. Take care of my cat this weekend.
10. Do my homework for me.

GO TO MyEnglishLab *FOR MORE GRAMMAR PRACTICE.*

PRONUNCIATION

1 🎧 Listen to the examples.

INTONATION IN QUESTIONS AND STATEMENTS

Our intonation can rise or fall at the end of a sentence. Our intonation helps listeners to understand the type of question we are asking and to understand when we have completed a sentence or statement.

Yes-No Questions	
Your voice falls to a low note and then rises to a high note at the end of the question.	🎧 Do you have the time?
	🎧 Could you hold the door for me, please?
Wh- Questions (who, what, where, when, why, how)	
Your voice rises on the important word at the end of a question, and then it falls to a low note.	🎧 What time is the movie?
	🎧 Where do you want to meet?

Statements

Your voice rises on the important word at the end of a statement, and then it falls to a low note.

🎧 I'd be happy to.

🎧 Sorry, I can't.

2 🎧 Listen to the questions. Draw lines to show where your voice rises and falls at the end. Then listen again and repeat the questions.

1. Would you help me?

2. Is this seat taken?[1]

3. Can I borrow your book, please?

4. Are you going to the party on Saturday?

5. Do you have the time?

6. How much money do you make?

7. What happened to your date?

8. Where did you learn manners?

3 🎧 Listen to the statements and repeat them. Make your voice rise and then fall at the end.

1. Certainly.
2. Sorry, but I'm using it.
3. I'd rather not say.[2]
4. From my parents.
5. Yeah, I'm looking forward to it.
6. It's four-thirty.
7. No, go ahead.
8. She called it off.

4 Work with a partner. Practice putting the questions from exercise 2 together with an appropriate response from exercise 3. Pay attention to your intonation.

---

[1] You can use this question when there is an empty seat next to someone who is sitting.
[2] You can use this statement to respond to a question that you would prefer not to answer.

SPEAKING SKILL

MAKING POLITE OFFERS AND INVITATIONS

There are different ways to make offers and invitations. There are also different ways to accept (say "yes") and to decline (say "no" or turn down the invitation).

Making Polite Offers and Invitations	Accepting and Declining
1. When making an offer, you can use polite questions with *would you like*: Would you like something to drink? Would you like some help?	 Yes, I would. Yes, thank you. Yes, please.
2. We can also make offers in less formal ways: Help yourself to a drink. Do you need any help?	 Thanks, I appreciate it. No, thanks. I'm good.
3. We can use polite questions with *would like* to invite someone to do something: Would you like to go to a movie?	I'd love to. Sure. That sounds great. I don't know. I need to check my schedule. Sorry, but I have to study tonight. Can we take a rain check?

Go around the class. Use the following information to make polite offers and invitations to your classmates. When you decline an invitation, be sure to give a reason.

Example

A: *Would you like something to drink?*

B: *No, thanks. I'm good.*

Offer your classmates:

1. something to drink

2. some chocolate

3. help on their homework

4. a ride home from school

Invite your classmates to:

1. go to a concert tonight

2. come to your house for dinner on Saturday

3. play soccer after class

4. go mountain climbing this summer

■■■■■■■■■■■■■■■ *GO TO* MyEnglishLab *FOR MORE SKILL PRACTICE AND TO CHECK WHAT YOU LEARNED.*

FINAL SPEAKING TASK

A role play is a short performance. The actors take on roles, or become characters, and act out a situation. The situations are often similar to experiences that people might have in real life.

In this task, you will discuss a situation, then prepare a three- to five-minute role play that relates to manners. Try to use the vocabulary, grammar, pronunciation, and language for making polite offers and invitations that you learned in the unit.*

Work in a group of three. Follow the steps.

STEP 1: Read each situation aloud in your group. Discuss the situations. What could you say?

1. You are in a restaurant having dinner with a friend. A person is sitting alone at a table near you, talking loudly on a cell phone. You can't hear your friend or enjoy your meal.

2. You are at a party with your friend. Another person comes over and enters the conversation and makes small talk with you. Your friend gets bored and starts texting.

3. You go to your friend's house for dinner. Your friend is from another culture. When you enter, you forget to take off your shoes. Then, during dinner, your friend's mother offers you different kinds of food that you never tried before. There is one kind of food that you don't like, but your friend's mother keeps offering it to you.

4. You bought expensive tickets to see a concert. You invite your friend to go with you. Your friend turns you down, but you don't believe the reason.

STEP 2: Choose one situation and prepare a role play.

STEP 3: Role-play your situation for the class.

---

*For Alternative Speaking Topics, see page 93.

Listen to each group's role play. Complete the chart.

SITUATION	RESPONSE	DO YOU AGREE WITH THE RESPONSE? WHY?

UNIT PROJECT

You will conduct a study like the one you heard about in Listening One.

STEP 1: Prepare for your study:

A. Go online to get some information about how to do a study. Find out how many people you should test to make it a good study. Look at some example studies to learn different ways you can report your results. For example, find some examples of different kinds of graphs or charts you can use to summarize the results of your study.

B. Work in groups of three. Divide the task. One student will do a door test, another student will do the document drop, and another student will do the customer service test.

C. Decide where you will go to do your study. If possible, go to a local café or a public place that has a variety of customers, such as students and business people.

D. Plan what you will do and what you will say during your study. Plan some polite questions you can ask during the customer service test, such as "Could I have a small coffee, please?" Practice your requests to be sure you use the correct grammar and intonation.

STEP 2: Conduct your study. Take turns conducting each part of the study. When one student is doing a test, the other students watch and take notes.

STEP 3: Fill in the chart with your results. Then compare your results to the results in Listening One. Are your results the same or different? Why do you think you got the results you did?

STEP 4: Present your results to the class. Are your results similar to or different from those of other students? Explain.

DESCRIBE THE PERSON	DOOR TEST:	DOCUMENT DROP:	CUSTOMER SERVICE:
(student, business person, etc.)	What did the person do? What did the person say?	What did the person do? What did the person say?	What did the person do? What did the person say? ("Can I help you?" "Thank you." etc.)

ALTERNATIVE SPEAKING TOPICS

Work in a small group. Read and discuss the quotes below. What do they mean to you? Explain each quote in your own words. Do you agree or disagree with the quote? Explain.

"Treat everyone with politeness, even those who are rude to you—not because they are nice, but because you are."—Author Unknown

"Consideration for others is the basis of a good life, a good society."—Confucius

"Visitors should behave in such a way that the host and hostess feel at home."—J.S. Farynski

■■■■■■■■■■■■■■■■■■■■■■■■■■ GO TO MyEnglishLab TO DISCUSS ONE OF THE ALTERNATIVE TOPICS, WATCH A VIDEO ABOUT ETIQUETTE, AND TAKE THE UNIT 4 ACHIEVEMENT TEST. ■■■■■■■■■■■■■■■■

THE FAT
Tax

1 FOCUS ON THE TOPIC

1. Look at the photo of the fast food. Do you think this food is healthy or unhealthy? Why? What are some other kinds of fast food that you know?

2. Our eating habits mean the foods and ways we usually eat. What are some unhealthy eating habits? What are some problems caused by unhealthy eating habits?

3. Look at the title of the unit. What do you think it means?

GO TO MyEnglishLab TO CHECK WHAT YOU KNOW.

VOCABULARY

1 🎧 Read and listen to the beginning of a radio show.

About 11 percent of the food Americans eat comes from fast food restaurants. And a lot of the food at fast food restaurants is **junk food**: soda, hamburgers, French fries—unhealthy foods that are high in salt, sugar, and fat. Many studies show that our **consumption** of junk food is related to one of the biggest **public health** problems in the United States today: the **increase** in **obesity**. People who are obese are extremely overweight—they weigh at least 20 percent more than what they should for their body type and height. And one of the main reasons that people are obese is because they eat too much fast food. To put it simply, Americans are too fat, and it is making them sick. Obesity causes some serious diseases, such as heart disease, diabetes, and some kinds of cancer. Obesity also costs a lot of money—in the billions of dollars a year in health care costs.

So how can we change our eating habits and **reduce** our consumption of junk food? For example, should the government put a **tax** on unhealthy foods to make them cost more? How can obese people **get rid of** the extra pounds that are slowly killing them? Do workplace programs to help people **lose weight** really help? Many programs **claim** to have the solution, but do they work? Can the government do anything to **discourage** Americans from eating so much junk food? What are the best ways to **deal with** the increase in obesity in the U.S.? That is the topic of today's show. We hope you will join the conversation, either by telephone or by joining our online discussion group.

2 Match the words on the left with the definitions on the right.

_____ **1.** junk food

_____ **2.** consumption

_____ **3.** public health

_____ **4.** obesity

_____ **5.** increase

_____ **6.** reduce

_____ **7.** discourage

_____ **8.** get rid of

_____ **9.** lose weight

_____ **10.** claim

_____ **11.** deal with

_____ **12.** tax

a. suggest that someone not do something

b. the condition of being extremely fat

c. remove or throw away something you do not want

d. food that is unhealthy

e. make the amount of size of something less than it was before

f. eating or using something

g. become greater in size, amount, number, etc.

h. say that something is true, even though it might not be

i. money people are required to pay the government

j. become thinner

k. the general physical condition of the citizens of a country

l. do something to solve a problem

■■■■■■■■■■■■■■■■■■■■■■■■■■■■■■■■■■■ GO TO MyEnglishLab FOR MORE VOCABULARY PRACTICE.

PREVIEW

Listen to the introduction to a radio show. Check (✓) two topics that the speakers are likely to discuss during the radio show.

_____ serious diseases such as cancer

_____ people's eating habits

_____ taxes on unhealthy food

_____ table manners

_____ ways to lose weight

MAIN IDEAS

1 🎧 Listen to the whole radio show. Look again at your predictions from the Preview section. Were any of your predictions correct? Did your predictions help you understand the story?

2 Circle the correct answers.

1. What is a fat tax?

   a. It is a tax on people who are obese.

   b. It is a tax on unhealthy foods that can make people obese.

   c. It is a tax on fast food restaurants that serve junk food.

2. What is the purpose of a fat tax?

   a. To discourage people from eating food that can make them obese.

   b. To pay for public health programs.

   c. To make fast food restaurants stop serving unhealthy food.

3. Which countries already tried a fat tax?

   a. The United States and Great Britain (the United Kingdom).

   b. Most European countries.

   c. Two countries in Europe.

4. Why did the government in Denmark get rid of the fat tax?

   a. The tax did not improve public health.

   b. The tax made food too expensive.

   c. The tax was not high enough.

5. Do fat taxes work?

   a. There is not enough information yet to say for sure.

   b. Probably not.

   c. Yes they do, but businesses don't like them.

DETAILS

Listen to the radio report again. Then read each statement. Write **T** *(true)* or **F** *(false)*. Then correct the false statements.

_____ 1. Roberta Anderson is a food researcher.

_____ 2. Fat taxes only raise the price of junk food.

_____ 3. Hungary got rid of its fat tax.

_____ 4. Shoppers and business owners in Denmark disagreed with the fat tax.

_____ 5. People from Denmark shopped in Germany because the food was better there.

_____ 6. Studies show that a fat tax in the United States might help people lose weight.

_____ 7. One study showed that a 20 percent tax on soda could reduce obesity by 3.5 percent.

_____ 8. A tax on pizza and soda could help Americans lose up to 18 percent of their body weight.

_____ 9. The fat tax may be one of the reasons that the consumption of butter, margarine, and oil went down in Denmark.

_____ 10. The economy[1] in Denmark was strong when the fat tax was introduced.

---

[1] **economy:** the system by which a country's money and business is organized

■■■■■■■■■■■■■■■■■■■■■■■■■■■■■■■■■■■■■■■ *GO TO* MyEnglishLab *FOR MORE LISTENING PRACTICE.*

MAKE INFERENCES

HEDGING

An inference is an educated guess about something that is not directly stated. To make an inference, use information that you understand from what you hear.

Reporters are careful about the words they choose because their job is to report the facts. As a result, they often use *hedges*. Hedges are phrases and words that people use to avoid expressing an opinion. People also hedge to avoid making a statement about something that is not certain. From the language and the tone of voice that someone uses, you can infer that he/she is hedging.

🎧 Listen to the example. Listen to the words and the tone of voice. What does the reporter mean?

Example

HOST: Do you mean that they got rid of the tax because of the costs, not public health?

REPORTER: Well, yes—at least that's what many people believe.

In the example, the speaker uses the words "at least that's what many people believe" to hedge. Although she says "yes," you can infer by her tone of voice and the words she uses—"at least" and "many people believe"—that she is avoiding expressing her own opinion; she is just reporting what others are saying.

🎧 Listen to the excerpts. What does the reporter mean? Circle the correct answer.

Excerpt One

    a. The reporter disagrees with what the researchers claim.

    b. The effect of the taxes is not certain yet, so the reporter does not want to say that taxes will make a difference.

Excerpt Two

    a. The reporter is saying that consumption of unhealthy food went down.

    b. The reporter is saying the fat tax caused people to eat less junk food.

EXPRESS OPINIONS

Work with two other students. Answer the questions. Give reasons for your opinions.

    1. Do you think a fat tax is a good idea? Why or why not?

    2. If some food costs more because there is a fat tax, will you still buy it? Why or why not?

    3. Do you think a fat tax is the best way to deal with the public health problem of obesity? Why or why not?

    4. What other ideas do you have for dealing with obesity?

■■■■■■■■■■■■■■■■■■■■■■■■■■ GO TO MyEnglishLab TO GIVE YOUR OPINION ABOUT ANOTHER QUESTION.

VOCABULARY

Read the words and expressions in the box aloud. Then read the sentences and circle the letter of the answer that best explains the meaning of the boldfaced word(s).

absolutely	be concerned about	take steps
affect	be in favor of	

1. **A:** Do you like Thai food?
   B: Absolutely! It's my favorite kind of food.

   a. Maybe.

   b. Yes, very much.

2. Please don't cry! There is nothing to **be concerned about**.

   a. worried about

   b. interested in

3. I **am in favor of** classes on healthy eating in all schools. It is important that all children grow up with healthy eating habits.

   a. like the idea of

   b. am worried about

4. The food you eat can **affect** your health. That's why you should eat food that's good for you.

   a. make a change in something

   b. make someone healthier

5. You need to **take steps** to improve your eating habits. Here is a list of things you can do.

   a. do something specific

   b. spend a lot of time

GO TO MyEnglishLab FOR MORE VOCABULARY PRACTICE.

COMPREHENSION

🎧 Listen to the second part of the radio show. Listeners call in with their opinions. Check (✓) the opinions that are true for each caller.

Caller One:

_____ Too many adults are obese.

_____ Obesity is a public health emergency.

_____ I'm in favor of a fat tax.

_____ Cigarette taxes didn't help reduce smoking.

Caller Two:

_____ Fat taxes are not a good idea.

_____ The government shouldn't control the food people eat.

_____ The government shouldn't be concerned with public health.

_____ Children should take steps to get rid of obesity.

_____ Parents need to teach their children about healthy eating.

_____ Schools need to educate students about healthy eating habits.

LISTENING SKILL

CLARIFYING

People sometimes need to ask for clarification—that is, they check to make sure that they understand what the speaker is saying or ask the speaker to repeat. Sometimes speakers repeat the information they heard, sometimes they ask questions, and sometimes they use certain expressions to ask for clarification. Listening for these expressions can help you to know that the speaker will confirm the meaning or explain more. If you didn't understand the speaker's point the first time, you will get a second chance to understand.

🎧 Listen to the example.

Example

HOST: So, if I understand correctly, a fat tax makes unhealthy foods more expensive, and then fewer people buy them?

ROBERTA ANDERSON: Yes, exactly—the idea is to discourage people from buying food that can make them obese.

In this example, the host checks his understanding of the fat tax. He signals to the reporter that he wants to clarify by saying, "So, if I understand correctly . . ." Then he uses rising intonation at the end of his statement: "A fat tax makes unhealthy foods more expensive, and then fewer people buy them?" This rising intonation signals to the reporter that he is checking his understanding. The reporter answers, "Yes, exactly," to confirm that his understanding is correct.

🎧 Listen to excerpts from *The Nation Talks*. Write what the speaker says to clarify. Then listen for the first speaker's response. Did the second speaker understand correctly? Check if the understanding was correct or incorrect.

Excerpt One

Clarification: _____? _____?

Speaker Two's Understanding: Correct / Incorrect

Excerpt Two

Clarification: _____ taxing unhealthy food will change people's eating habits that much?

Speaker Two's Understanding: Correct / Incorrect

Excerpt Three

Clarification: Sorry. _____ you just _____ . . . ?

Speaker Two's Understanding: Correct / Incorrect

■■ *GO TO* MyEnglishLab *FOR MORE SKILL PRACTICE.*

CONNECT THE LISTENINGS

STEP 1: Organize

🎧 Listen to excerpts from Listenings One and Two. Complete the chart with information you hear.

	TAX ON WHAT?	HOW MUCH?	RESULT?
BRITISH STUDY			*Obesity reduced by 3.5%*
U.S. STUDY		*18%*	
1990S TAX	*cigarettes*	*Cigarette cost increased by 50%*	

Work with a partner. Student A, you are a host on a radio show. Student B, you are a reporter. You are talking about how taxes can change people's behavior. Complete the conversation by using information from the chart above.

Example

A: So can you explain how taxes can change people's behavior?

B: Sure. For example, a British study shows that if you add a _____ tax on _____, you can reduce _____ by 3.5 percent.

A: Really? That's a lot!

B: Yes, but remember, it is just a study.

Now switch roles and talk about a different tax. You will need to change the conversation a little bit for each type of tax.

■■ *GO TO* MyEnglishLab *TO CHECK WHAT YOU LEARNED.*

3 FOCUS ON SPEAKING

VOCABULARY

REVIEW

Use the words and expressions in the box to complete the discussions. Then practice the discussions with a partner.

Discussion 1: Two parents at a meeting

absolutely	discourage	junk food
concerned about	get rid of	obesity
deal with	in favor of	

A: Can you believe that there are vending machines at the school that sell soda and other

_____, like chips and candy?
　　　1.

B: Really? That's crazy!

A: Yeah, I think so too. It's sending the wrong message. I'm really _____ it.
2.

B: Well, why don't we do something? Can't we try and get the schools to remove the

machines—just _____ them completely? I think most parents would be
3.

_____ that, don't you?
4.

A: Yes, _____! We all know that kids drink too much soda and eat too
5.

much junk food. And it's really bad for their health. Just look at the problems of

_____ among young people in this country today. So many of our kids
6.

are just too fat, and it's making them sick.

B: Yes, and selling soda and junk food at school sends the wrong message. How

can we teach kids healthy eating habits when they can go right down the hallway

and buy junk food and soda? It's crazy! Schools need to do everything they can

to _____ kids from eating junk food. And if the schools won't
7.

_____ the problem, then we as parents need to do something.
8.

A: OK, so what should we do? What's our first step?

B: Why don't we start by calling the principal of the school? We can make an

appointment to talk to him about our concerns.

A: That's a great idea. Let's do it!

Discussion 2: Radio call-in show

affect	consumption	lose weight	reduce

A: Hello? Go ahead—you're on *The Nation Talks*.

B: Yes? My name is Mary, and I wanted to say something about what the caller before me

was saying. You know, the caller who was talking about cigarette taxes and how they

really helped _____ the sale of cigarettes?

1.

A: Yes. So what is the point you would like to make?

B: Well, I don't think you can really compare food and cigarettes. Overweight people

who need to _____ are very different from smokers.

2.

A: What do you mean? Could you be a little more specific?

B: Of course. Smokers don't *need* to smoke, but people do need to eat—even people

who are overweight or obese. That's why food taxes won't really _____

3.

people's behavior. If you tax one food, you might lower the _____ of

4.

that particular food, but people will just find something else to eat.

A: So how can we deal with the problem of obesity?

B: I believe that people need to take personal responsibility for their weight problems.

That is the only thing that will work.

A: OK, well thank you very much for your call.

Read the brochure. Pay attention to the words in boldface.

(5) STEPS TO HEALTHY EATING

1. Don't **go on a diet**! People who go on diets might lose weight at first, but as soon as they stop dieting, they not only **gain** back everything they lost, but often gain extra weight.

2. Become a more colorful eater—fruits and vegetables that are bright and colorful are especially good for you. Dark green, blue, purple, and red fruits and vegetables are good choices. Colorful foods taste great and will give you lots of energy.

| broccoli | spinach | blueberries | cabbage | eggplant | beets | tomatoes |

3. Watch your **portion** size by using small bowls and plates. Try the "healthy plate" model. Fill half your plate with salad or vegetables. Fill one-quarter of it with some kind of **protein**—fish, seafood, beans, meat, eggs, tofu, or chicken (without the skin). Fill the final quarter with **whole-grain** bread or cereal, rice, pasta, or potatoes.

Proteins

| beans | tofu | fish | meat | eggs | Whole Grains |

4. Eat your biggest meals early in the day. Research shows you burn more **calories** if you eat earlier in the day than if you eat in the evening. And eating a good, healthy breakfast, including fresh fruit and protein (yogurt, eggs, cottage cheese) starts your day off right. Just like a car needs gas to move, your body needs energy early in the day.

5. Be smart with snacks. You don't need to **give up** snacks—just choose healthy ones, such as **raw** carrots, cauliflower, or celery, a tablespoon of raw nuts, a piece of fruit, or yogurt or cottage cheese with whole-grain crackers.

| carrots | cauliflower | celery | nuts | yogurt | cottage cheese |

Write the word or phrase in boldface from the brochure next to the correct definition.

1. _____   not cooked

2. _____   stop doing something that you have done a lot

3. _____   energy that you get from food

4. _____   a substance in food such as meat or eggs that helps your body
                        to grow and be healthy

5. _____   to become heavier

6. _____   made using all parts of the seed of a plant, such as rice or wheat

7. _____   an amount of food for one person

8. _____   eat less food and different kinds of food in order to lose weight

CREATE

Work with a partner to prepare a role play. A role play is a short performance. The actors take on roles, or become characters, and act out a situation. The situations are often similar to experiences that people might have in real life.

STUDENT A: You are a counselor who works with people who are trying to develop healthier eating habits. Ask Student B some questions to find out about his/her eating habits. Then give some advice.

STUDENT B: You are tired a lot of the time. You are visiting a counselor because you want advice on how to improve your eating habits so that you will have more energy and feel better. Answer Student A's questions.

Get started like this:

STUDENT A: So how can I help you today?

STUDENT B: Well, lately I feel really tired all of the time.

List of possible questions

How many meals do you usually eat a day?

What do you eat for breakfast? Lunch? Dinner?

Do you eat a lot of snacks during the day? What kinds of snacks do you eat?

What is your biggest meal of the day?

Where do you eat? At home? At restaurants? At your desk? In the car?

Do you eat a lot of fast food?

Who do you eat with? Family? Friends? Alone?

Use the questions in the list (as well as your own ideas), information and vocabulary from the brochure, and the vocabulary from Listenings One and Two. Then find a new partner. Switch roles and perform the role play again.

▪▫▪▫▪▫▪▫▪▫▪▫▪▫▪▫▪▫▪▫▪▫▪▫▪▫▪▫▪▫▪▫▪▪ *GO TO* MyEnglishLab *FOR MORE VOCABULARY PRACTICE.*

GRAMMAR

MODALS OF POSSIBILITY	
1. Use *might*, *may* and *could* to express **possibility** about the present or future.	Several studies show that fat taxes **might work**. Fat taxes **may help** change consumers' eating habits. Fat taxes **could help** reduce obesity.
2. *Might*, *may* and *could* are followed by the base form of the verb.	A fat tax **might work**. NOT: A fat tax might ~~works~~. NOT: A fat tax might ~~to work~~.
3. The **negative of possibility** in the present or future is *may not* or *might not*. There are no contractions for *may* or *might*. Do NOT use *could not* for the negative of possibility. *Could not* means **impossible** in the PAST. Use *may not* or *might not*.	A fat tax **might/may not work**. = 50% possibility it won't work (so 50% possibility it will work) NOT: A fat tax ~~mightn't~~ work. He **could not change** his eating habits. = It was impossible for him to change his eating habits. (0 percent chance)
4. We use *may*, *might* or *could* for something that is **possible**, but **not certain**. We use *will* for something that is **certain**, or that **we think is certain**.	Taxes **might make** a difference in what people eat. If there is a fat tax, people **will pay** it. They won't have any other choice.

(continued on next page)

5. We use *I think* + **subject** + *might* for possibility. We use *I'm sure* + **subject** + *will* for certainty.	**I think a fat tax might** work. **I'm sure business owners will** be unhappy about a fat tax. NOT: I'm sure business owners ~~might~~ be unhappy about a fat tax.
We use *I think* + **subject** + *will* for something that is likely.	**I think the government will** introduce a fat tax this year.
6. *May* and *might* are modals. *Maybe* is an adverb. It means "there's a possibility."	**Maybe** people **will lose** weight = People **might lose** weight. or People **may lose** weight. or People **could lose** weight.
If you use the adverb *maybe*, use **will** with the main verb. Do NOT use *might, may,* or *could*.	**Maybe** the fat tax **will** work. NOT: Maybe the fat tax ~~might~~ work.

1 Complete the sentences. Choose the correct answer.

1. My son is overweight, and my doctor is concerned that he _____ obese.

   a. maybe become   **b.** could become   **c.** might becomes

2. Many people think that going on a diet _____ them lose weight, but they are wrong.

   a. maybe will help   **b.** will help   **c.** may to help

3. Fat taxes _____, but I think they are a good idea. The government needs to do something to deal with obesity in this country.

   a. mightn't to work   **b.** couldn't work   **c.** may not work

4. If junk food is taxed, maybe fewer people _____ it.

   a. will buy   **b.** might buy   **c.** may not buy

5. Eating healthy snacks like raw vegetables between meals _____ you to eat smaller portions at mealtimes.

   a. might to help   **b.** might helps   **c.** might help

6. I am sure that you _____ weight if you reduce the number of calories that you consume every day.

   a. might lose   **b.** will lose   **c.** could lose

2 Work in groups of three. Take turns talking about possibilities.

Example

STUDENT A: I'm trying to lose weight. **Maybe I'll go** on a diet.

STUDENT B: Really? **Are you sure a diet will** work? I think that people on diets often gain weight again after a while.

STUDENT C: That's true. Why don't you try the 5 Steps Program we learned about in health class last week? That **might work** better for you than a diet.

1. Your friend eats fast food all of the time and gets sick a lot. He/she isn't overweight, but you are concerned that his/her eating habits are not healthy. Talk about some things he/she might do.

2. Your city has a big problem with obesity. Talk about some steps the government might take to deal with the problem.

3. You are a parent, and you want your children to grow up with healthy eating habits. Talk about what you might do.

4. You are a school principal and many of the children in your school have unhealthy eating habits and eat a lot of junk food. Talk about the steps that you might take to discourage unhealthy eating habits in the school.

GO TO MyEnglishLab FOR MORE GRAMMAR PRACTICE.

PRONUNCIATION

INTONATION ON CLARIFICATION QUESTIONS

When we ask information questions, our intonation falls at the end. But when we ask questions for clarification or repetition, our voice rises at the end. This signals to the speaker to repeat the same information.

Listen to the conversations. Repeat the intonation patterns that you see and hear.

1. **A:** How does the fat tax work?

   B: It increases the tax on unhealthy foods.

2. **A:** *How* does it work?

   B: I said it increases the tax on unhealthy food.

In the first question, Speaker A used falling intonation to ask for information about the fat tax. In the second question, Speaker A used rising intonation to ask for repetition. Notice how Speaker A also stresses the word "How" to show that is the part of the question that needs to be repeated.

We also use rising intonation on statements to ask for clarification:

3. **A:** A fat tax increases the cost of the food.

   B: So, you're saying it makes it more expensive?

   A: Yes, exactly.

Work with a partner. Take turns. Student A, make a statement. Student B, respond using rising intonation to ask for repetition or falling intonation to ask for more information. Then Student A chooses an appropriate response

1. **A:** I just ate lunch.

   B: What did you eat?

   a. Lunch.   **b.** I had a hamburger and chips.

2. **A:** I'm starting a new diet next week.

   B: When?

   a. Next week.   **b.** On Monday.

3. **A:** I'm taking a trip to Germany.

   B: Where are you taking a trip?

   a. Germany.   **b.** Berlin.

4. **A:** I met a reporter today.

   B: Who did you meet?

   a. A reporter.   **b.** Roberta Anderson.

SPEAKING SKILL

ASKING FOR CLARIFICATION OR REPETITION

In conversation, when we don't understand the other speaker, we need to *clarify*, or check our understanding. Sometimes we also need to ask the speaker to repeat what was said. There are different ways to ask for clarification or repetition.

Clarification: Some common expressions

ASKING FOR CLARIFICATION	CLARIFYING
I'm sorry, I'm not following you . . .	
I didn't catch that.	
Use rising intonation to check your understanding:	
Are you saying that . . . ?	Yes/yeah/, exactly—
You mean to say that . . . ?	No, I'm saying that . . .
Do you mean that . . . ?	Actually, I mean . . .
Use falling intonation to ask for more information:	
What do you mean by . . . ?	I mean . . .
How do you spell that . . . ?	It's spelled . . .

ASKING FOR REPETITION	REPEATING
Use rising intonation to ask for repetition:	
Excuse me?	I said . . .
Sorry?	Sure . . .
What did you just say?	(I went) to the supermarket with my roommate to get some fruit.
Sorry, could you say that again?	
You went *where*?	(I went) to the supermarket.
What did you buy?	(I bought) some fruit.
Who did you go with?	(I went) with my roommate.

Work with a partner. Take turns explaining something. Use the ideas from the list, or come up with your own. Use the language in the chart to ask for and give clarification. Try to use the rising and falling intonation patterns that you practiced in the Pronunciation section.

Example

A: Could you please tell me about a popular meal in your country?

B: Yes, of course. Arroz con pollo is probably the most typical dish in my country.

A: I'm sorry, I didn't catch that. What's the name of the dish?

B: Arroz con pollo.

A: I'm sorry I'm not following you. Could you spell that for me?

B: Sure, it's A-R-R-O-Z C-O-N P-O-L-L-O. It means rice with chicken in English.

Explain . . .

a popular dish (type of food) from your country.

polite table manners in your country.

how eating habits in your country are different from eating habits in the United States. (or another country you are familiar with)

a problem in your country today.

▪▪▪▪▪▪▪▪▪▪▪▪▪▪▪ *GO TO* MyEnglishLab *FOR MORE SKILL PRACTICE AND TO CHECK WHAT YOU LEARNED.*

FINAL SPEAKING TASK

In a debate, two teams discuss different sides of the same topic. One team is pro (for) a statement, and the other team is con (against) the same statement.

In this activity, you will prepare a debate about the role of the government in reducing obesity. Try to use the vocabulary, grammar, pronunciation, and language for clarification that you learned in the unit.*

Follow the steps.

STEP 1: Your teacher will divide the class into two or more teams to debate the following statement:

STATEMENT: The government should take whatever steps are necessary to reduce obesity.

Team A = PRO side   You will argue in favor of the statement.

Team B = CON side   You will argue against the statement.

PRO: The government must protect the public health

> I need to take whatever steps are necessary to save people's lives. People are dying every day because of obesity, and we need to do something about it.

---

*For Alternative Speaking Topics, see page 117.

CON: The government has no right to tell people what to do

STEP 2: Meet with your team to prepare for the debate:

- Choose a group leader.
- Plan your arguments (ideas in favor of your opinion). You can use ideas you learned from the unit and your own ideas. Takes notes.
- Think about the possible arguments that the other team may make. Plan your counter-arguments (points you use against the other team's arguments).

Example

Other team's argument: The fat tax probably won't work. People may go somewhere else to buy unhealthy foods.

Counter-argument: Some people will change their eating habits. Research shows the fat tax could work just like the cigarette tax worked to reduce smoking.

STEP 3: Debate the topic with another team. The two teams take turns presenting their arguments and counter-arguments. The teacher is the moderator who invites people to speak. Make sure each member of your team presents at least one argument or counter-argument. The group leaders make the closing statements for each team. In the closing statement, the leader briefly summarizes the main points for each team.

Listening Task

Listen to each team's arguments and counter-arguments and take notes. Which team made a more convincing argument? Why?

UNIT PROJECT

STEP 1: Research on the Internet to find out about obesity and eating habits in a different country. Choose a country that has either a large number of obese people or a low number of obese people.

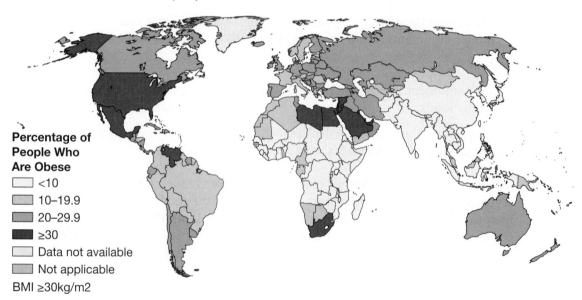

Percentage of People Who Are Obese

- <10
- 10–19.9
- 20–29.9
- ≥30
- Data not available
- Not applicable

BMI ≥30kg/m2

STEP 2: Research the eating habits of the people in that country on the Internet or in the library. Use the questions to help you in your research.

1. Where is this country?

2. How many people are overweight? How many are obese?

3. What kinds of foods do people usually eat? Which foods are the most popular? Do they eat fast food?

4. What are their eating habits? For example, how often do they eat? What time of day do they eat? Where do they eat? How long do they spend cooking and eating?

5. What are some other interesting facts about _____?

STEP 3: Think about the information you found.

Why do you think people are obese or not obese in this country?

What can we learn from the eating habits of the people in this country?

What might people in this country do to have healthier diets?

STEP 4: Share your information with the class.

ALTERNATIVE SPEAKING TOPICS

Work in a group. Discuss the questions.

1. Describe the usual eating habits of people in your country, for example:
   - How many meals do most people eat a day, and at what times? Which meal is the most important meal of the day?
   - What kinds of food do people usually eat? Home-cooked? Take out? Fast food?
   - Where do people usually eat their meals? At home? In restaurants?
   - Who do people usually eat with? With family members or friends? Alone?

2. Do you enjoy eating foods from different countries? Which country's food (other than your own) do you like best? Why do you like it?

3. Do you think fast food can be healthy? Why or why not? Give an example of a fast food and explain why you think it is healthy or unhealthy.

4. What's your favorite food? Why do you like it? Is it healthy or unhealthy?

■■■■■■■■■■■■■■■■■■■■■■■■■■■■■ *GO TO* MyEnglishLab *TO DISCUSS ONE OF THE ALTERNATIVE TOPICS,*
WATCH A VIDEO ABOUT A FOOD COMPANY, AND TAKE THE UNIT 5 ACHIEVEMENT TEST. ■■■■■■■■■■■■■■■

EVERYDAY
Heroes

1. Look at the photo. What is happening?

2. What does the word *hero* mean to you?

3. Can you think of any famous heroes? What do you think an "everyday hero" is?

2 FOCUS ON LISTENING

LISTENING ONE | THE SUBWAY HERO

VOCABULARY

1 🎧 Read and listen to the student presentation about heroes.

What Does It Take to Be a Hero?

We can all think of heroes in our lives. But, did you ever think about what it really takes to be a hero? What does someone have to do to become a hero? Well, in my opinion, there are four characteristics of a hero.

First of all, heroes help others in need. For example, a hero may help someone in a dangerous situation. Or, a hero may provide a service to people who live in their **community** who need help.

In addition, heroes make the choice to help out because they want to, not because it is required or because someone told them to do it.

Third, heroes help others even when there are **risks**. This means that heroes will help even in situations where there is a chance that they will get hurt or something bad will happen to them as a result of their actions.

Finally, heroes help others even when there is no reward for their actions. They don't do good things because they want to get something for themselves in return. They just help because they believe it is **the right thing** to do.

For example, take the story of Laurie Eldridge. One day, Ms. Eldridge was outside in her garden, when she looked up and saw a car stuck on some nearby train tracks. Inside the car was an 81-year-old woman who didn't notice there was a train coming toward her. Ms. Eldridge **reacted** quickly. She ran to the car and pulled the woman out of it just before the train arrived. The car was destroyed, but it **turned out** that the woman, Angeline Pascucci, was OK.

Laurie Eldridge didn't think her actions were **brave**. She said she just did what any **ordinary** person would do. However, the people in her community disagreed. They **praised** her actions and gave her an award to thank her for her **courage**.

To me, Laurie Eldridge is a hero because she risked her own life to help someone else in need. In the end, she didn't expect anything for herself. Just knowing she helped another person was reward enough for her.

2 Write each boldfaced word or phrase from the text next to its definition or synonym.

_____ the ability to do something you know is difficult or dangerous

_____ behaved in a particular way when something happened

_____ ended

_____ a group of people who live in the same area

_____ possibilities that something bad will happen

_____ the correct or acceptable thing

_____ feeling or showing no fear; not afraid

_____ not unusual or special

_____ said good things about

■■■■■■■■■■■■■■■■■■■■■■■■■■■■■■■■■■■■ GO TO MyEnglishLab FOR MORE VOCABULARY PRACTICE.

PREVIEW

A news reporter is telling the story of an everyday hero.

subway platform and tracks

🎧 Listen to the beginning of the news program. What happened? What do you think will happen next? List three possible events.

1. _____

2. _____

3. _____

MAIN IDEAS

1 🎧 Listen to the whole program. Look again at your predictions from the Preview section. Were any of them correct? Did your predictions help you understand the story?

2 All of the statements contain some FALSE information. Cross out the parts that are untrue and write the correct information. Some statements can be corrected in more than one way.

Example

on the platform

Subway riders were waiting ~~on the train~~.

1. Cameron Hollopeter is a young woman who fell on the subway tracks.

2. Wesley Autrey was waiting on the platform with his teenage sons.

3. Wesley Autrey pulled Cameron Hollopeter back on to the platform.

4. The two men lay down on the tracks next to the subway train.

5. The train stopped before it passed over the two men.

6. Wesley Autrey thinks he is a hero.

DETAILS

🎧 Listen to the program again. Circle the best answer to complete each statement.

1. Cameron Hollopeter is a _____.

   a. high school student

   b. college student

   c. college teacher

2. Wesley Autrey is a _____ construction worker.

   a. 20-year-old

   b. 50-year-old

   c. 55-year-old

3. Wesley Autrey left his two daughters _____ on the platform.

   a. alone

   b. with a woman

   c. with his family

4. The train arrived _____ after Wesley Autrey jumped on to the tracks.

    a. two seconds

    b. six seconds

    c. six minutes

5. The subway train passed _____ above Mr. Autrey's head.

    a. less than an inch

    b. less than two inches

    c. less than a foot

6. Richard thinks that jumping on to the subway tracks was _____.

    a. brave

    b. crazy

    c. exciting

7. Emily thought about _____.

    a. Cameron Hollopeter

    b. Wesley Autrey

    c. Wesley Autrey's daughters

8. Wesley Autrey didn't worry about _____.

    a. his daughters

    b. being late for work

    c. getting hurt

9. Wesley Autrey said his _____ raised him to help people.

    a. mother

    b. father

    c. family

GO TO MyEnglishLab FOR MORE LISTENING PRACTICE.

MAKE INFERENCES

UNDERSTANDING A SPEAKER'S FEELINGS FROM TONE OF VOICE AND WORD CHOICE

An inference is a guess about something that is not directly stated. To make an inference, use information that you understand from what you hear.

We can often guess a speaker's feelings by the tone, or sound, of the speaker's voice. Our tone of voice shows how we are feeling, for example, if we are happy, sad, angry, surprised, or worried. We can also guess a speaker's feelings by the words that the speaker uses. For example, they may choose words that show that they are surprised or worried.

In this news program, the people being interviewed describe the feelings they had in the subway station.

Listen to the example. How did the speaker feel? What word best describes the speaker's tone of voice? Was she *surprised* or *worried*? What words does the speaker use to show this feeling?

Example

WOMAN 1: So, this guy was just lying there on the tracks, and he couldn't get up. And then I saw that a train was coming! . . . and then this man, I couldn't believe it . . . he just jumped down, right onto the tracks!

In this example, the speaker uses a *surprised* tone of voice. She also uses the words *I couldn't believe it* to show that the action surprised her.

Listen to three excerpts from the report. After listening to each excerpt, check the adjective that describes the speaker's tone of voice and take notes of words that show how the speaker was feeling.

Excerpt One

Tone of voice: Words to show feelings: _____

_____ surprised

_____ worried

Excerpt Two

Tone of voice: Words to show feelings: _____

_____ surprised

_____ worried

Excerpt Three

Tone of voice: Words to show feelings: _____

_____ surprised

_____ worried

EXPRESS OPINIONS

Discuss the questions with the class.

1. Can you understand why Wesley Autrey risked his life to save another man? Would you do it?

2. Do you think most people can do what Wesley Autrey did? Why or why not?

3. Do you think that people are born with courage, or can we learn to be brave?

■ GO TO MyEnglishLab TO GIVE YOUR OPINION ABOUT ANOTHER QUESTION.

LISTENING TWO   PSYCHOLOGY LECTURE—ALTRUISM

VOCABULARY

Read the words and phrases in the box. Then read the sentences and circle the best definition for the word in bold.

genes	responsible for	show concern for	unselfish	volunteer

1. My parents taught me to **show concern for** others. I learned to be kind to people and to help others in my community.

   a. be interested in and care about

   b. give help to

2. Charlie is lucky he was born with good **genes**. His parents were both very healthy and lived long lives.

   a. habits that parents teach their children

   b. small parts of cells that come from our parents and affect our characteristics

3. Parents are **responsible for** their children. Parents must be sure their children have food to eat and are safe and healthy.

   a. having the job or duty of taking care of someone or something

   b. having the job or duty of feeding someone or something

(continued on next page)

Everyday Heroes 125

4. My cousin Max is an **unselfish** person. For example, he always helps me with my schoolwork even though he is very busy.

    a. showing as much or more care for others as for yourself

    b. working hard to do well in school

5. In her free time, Young **volunteers** at a homeless shelter. She helps to clean and cook meals for the people staying there. She says she wants to do it because it makes her feel good to help others.

    a. to do work for others so they can live a better life

    b. to offer to do something without being forced to or without getting paid to do it

■■■■■■■■■■■■■■■■■■■■■■■■■■■■■■■ *GO TO* MyEnglishLab *FOR MORE VOCABULARY PRACTICE.*

COMPREHENSION

Listen to a psychology lecture on altruism. Fill in the missing information in the notes.

Psychology 101
Lecture 6
Altruism
Altruism = showing _____ for others (i.e.[1] caring for others, not thinking about _____)
   - _____ or simple acts (e.g.:[2] saving from _____ or holding door, giving _____)
   - Many ppl[3] don't _____: only _____ percent take risks to help

Why do some help & others don't?
Possible Factors:
  1) Situation
     More likely to help ppl we _____ (e.g., friends, family), not

     _____
     - " _____ "[4] when _____, not in crowd
  2) _____
     - Ppl w/[5]certain _____ help more than others
  3) Personality – kind of person (e.g., ppl w/ positive _____ more likely to help)
     - expect things will be _____
  4) Way we are _____
     - Parents teach some to be _____ for others

---

[1] **i.e.** = in other words   [4] "   " = repeat line above
[2] **e.g.** = for example   [5] **w/** = with
[3] **ppl** = people

LISTENING SKILL

UNDERSTANDING LECTURE SIGNAL PHRASES

In *lectures*, speakers use certain phrases to introduce the organization of the lecture and to signal new ideas. They use phrases to introduce a topic, list main points and signal transitions, or changes from one topic to another. Listening for these phrases can help you to follow the ideas in a lecture and help you to organize your notes.

🎧 Listen to these examples:

Example 1

In this example, the speaker introduces the topic of the lecture with the phrase: *Today, I'd like to talk about . . .* Then, she says the topic of the lecture: altruism.

Example 2

In this example, the speaker asks the question: *Why do some people help out and others don't?* to signal that she is moving to a new topic. Next, she answers the question: *We don't know for sure.*

The speaker also says: *The research shows several possible factors.* This phrase signals to us that we should listen for a list of factors.

🎧 Listen to excerpts from *Psychology Lecture: Altruism.* Listen to how the speaker uses phrases to introduce a main point or to make a transition to a new topic. Write the lecture phrase on the line, and then write the topic that it introduces.

Excerpt One

Lecture Phrase: _____

Idea or Topic: _____

Excerpt Two

Lecture Phrase: _____

Idea or Topic: _____

Excerpt Three

Lecture Phrase: _____

Idea or Topic: _____

Excerpt Four

Lecture Phrase: _____

Idea or Topic: _____

GO TO MyEnglishLab *FOR MORE SKILL PRACTICE.*

STEP 1: Organize

Complete the chart with specific examples from Listenings One and Two that support the general ideas about altruism from the lecture. Write the statements below in the correct places in the chart.

- ~~People with a certain gene are more likely to give money to people in need.~~
- ~~Wesley Autrey risked his life to save a man from being hit by a train.~~
- Wesley Autrey didn't worry about getting hit by the train.
- Wesley Autrey chose to jump onto the tracks to save the man.
- The other people on the platform didn't try to save the man.
- Wesley Autrey's mother raised him to help people when he could.

GENERAL IDEAS ON ALTRUISM FROM THE LECTURE	SPECIFIC EXAMPLES
What does altruism mean? 1. People show unselfish concern for others. 2. People volunteer to help others	1. _Wesley Autrey risked his life to save a man from being hit by a train._ 2. _____
Why do some people help others? 1. People are less likely to help when they are in a crowd. 2. Some people have genes that make them more likely to help. 3. Some people are raised to help others. 4. People with positive attitudes are more likely to help others.	1. _____ 2. _People with a certain gene are more likely to give money to those in need._ 3. _____ 4. _____

Work with a partner. Student A, you are a reporter interviewing a psychology professor about altruism. Ask your partner the questions in the chart. Ask follow-up questions to get more information. Student B, you are a psychology professor. Answer the reporter's questions using the information from Step 1.

Example

A: What does altruism mean?

B: Well, altruism is when people show unselfish concern for others.

A: OK. Can you give me an example?

B: Sure. Wesley Autrey showed unselfish concern when he risked his life to save a man from being hit by a train.

A: I see. So, what else can you tell us about altruism?

Switch roles and repeat the conversation.

GO TO MyEnglishLab TO CHECK WHAT YOU LEARNED.

VOCABULARY

REVIEW

Complete the magazine article with the words in the box.

community	praised	show concern for	turned out
courage	reacted	take risks	volunteer

ALTRUISM IN ANIMALS

1 Most discussions of altruism focus on people, but what about animals? Does altruism happen in the animal world? Actually, research shows that, in fact, animals may also _____ others.
   1.

2 For example, in one study, researchers found that female chimpanzees prefer to share their food rather than keep it for themselves. In the study, one chimp had three choices: feed a piece of banana to herself, feed herself and another chimp, or do nothing. It _____ that almost always, the chimps chose to share the bananas. Other studies with chimpanzees show that they often _____ to help each other in dangerous situations.
   2.
   3.

Scientists believe this shows that chimpanzees, like people, will choose to help others in their _____, even when they don't get a reward for their actions.
   4.

3 Another study at the University of Chicago found examples of unselfish behavior in rats. In this study, one rat was locked inside a small trap with a door. Another rat showed _____ by approaching the trap
   5.

and learning how to open the door to free the rat inside. In another test, the free rat was given some chocolate, but rather than eat the chocolate itself, it freed the other rat and shared the chocolate.

4 These studies show that animals will _____ to help their own kind,

      6.

but animals can also show concern for different kinds of animals or people. One famous example is Binti the gorilla. One day, a three-year-old boy fell down into the area where Binti lived with the other gorillas at the Brookfield Zoo. The boy was badly hurt and couldn't move. Instead of trying to hurt him, Binti _____ by helping the boy. She

      7.

carefully picked him up and carried him over to the door where a person could reach him and take him away. Many people were surprised and _____ Binti as a hero.

      8.

EXPAND

1 🎧 Read and listen to the interview with a real-life superhero.

A: So, tell me, what is a real-life superhero?

B: Well, real-life superheroes are ordinary people like me who **do good deeds** in our communities.

A: So there are others like you?

B: Oh yeah, there are many of us all around the world. We help people in need, and we try to stop crimes from happening.

A: But that sounds like work for the police. Why don't you just get a job as a police officer?

B: Well, I already have a job. I decided to volunteer as a real-life superhero in my free time because I saw too much crime in my community. I wanted **to get involved** and take action to stop it.

(continued on next page)

A: So you walk the streets trying to stop crime? Sounds dangerous. Aren't there safer ways to help out?

B: Well, sure. Many real-life superheroes prefer to help the poor or sick or work with volunteer groups. There are many ways to get involved and **make a difference** in our communities.

A: Stopping crime, helping others . . . all of these are **generous** things to do. It sounds like you **have a good heart**. But, I wonder, why do you wear a mask and a superhero costume? Why don't you just wear regular clothing?

B: That's a good question. For me, there are a few reasons. First of all, my costume helps people to **recognize** me. When people see me on the street, they know who I am and they come to me for help, and they often come up to thank me for the work I do. Kids especially love my costume. They are always so excited to see a real superhero.

A: OK, I see . . .

B: But more important, I want people to notice me because I want to **inspire** others to get involved in their communities too. Too many people these days just don't show concern for each other, or they don't know how they can help. I want to be a **role model** for others and encourage them to get out and **contribute** in any way they can. I often hear from people who say they **admire** me for being so brave and helping to make our community a better place to live. That's the best reward of all.

2 Match the words and phrases on the left with their meanings on the right.

_____ 1. contribute

_____ 2. do good deeds

_____ 3. get involved

_____ 4. generous

_____ 5. have a good heart

_____ 6. recognize

_____ 7. inspire

_____ 8. role model

_____ 9. admire

_____ 10. make a difference

a. to make someone want to do something

b. happy to give to or help others

c. a person looked to by others as an example to be followed.

d. to know and remember; to give special attention or notice to

e. to give something, such as money, time, or goods to a person or group

f. do something kind or helpful

g. have a positive effect

h. to feel respect or approval for someone or something

i. to be kind

j. participate in something

Work in a small group. Take turns asking and answering the questions. Use the boldfaced words and vocabulary from Review and Expand in your answers.

1. Do you think it is a good idea for real-life superheroes to **get involved** in their communities to stop crime? Do you think they **take** too many **risks**? Explain your answer.

2. Do you think we are **responsible** for caring for others in our community? Do you think one person can **make a difference** in other people's lives? Why or Why not?

3. Do you **volunteer** in your **community**? If not, what kind of volunteer work do you think your community needs the most?

4. Name a person you know who **is altruistic**. Why do you think this person likes to help others? Give an example of something this person did that was **generous** or shows they **have a good heart**.

5. Name a person you know who has **courage**. Why do you think this person is **brave**?

6. Name a person you think is a good **role model** for others. What does this person do to **inspire** others?

■■■■■■■■■■■■■■■■■■■■■■■■■■■■■■■■■■■ GO TO MyEnglishLab FOR MORE VOCABULARY PRACTICE.

GRAMMAR

1 Read the paragraph. Underline the verbs that talk about the past. Then answer the questions.

Last month I decided to start volunteering in my community. Yesterday I started my volunteer job at an animal shelter, where I learned how to care for homeless pets. At the end of the day, I was happy knowing I made a difference in their lives.

a. How is the past tense formed for most of the verbs (regular verbs)?

b. Which past tense verbs are irregular? What are the base forms for these verbs?

SIMPLE PAST TENSE	
1. We use the simple past tense to talk about actions that are finished.	Yesterday I *started* my volunteer job.
2. To form the simple past tense for **regular** verbs, add *-ed* to the base form of the verb.	Base form　　　　Simple Past *start*　　　　　*started*
If the verb ends in -*e*, add only *d*.	*decide*　　　　*decided*
If the verb ends in a consonant + *y*, change the *y* to *i* and then add *-ed*.	*try*　　　　　*tried*

(continued on next page)

3. Many verbs have **irregular** past tense forms. Here are some of the irregular verbs.	*be* *was/were*

be	*was/were*
come	*came*
do	*did*
fall	*fell*
go	*went*
have	*had*
hold	*held*
get	*got*
give	*gave*
make	*made*
meet	*met*
see	*saw*
take	*took*
win	*won*

4. In negative statements, use ***did not*** + *base form*. Use ***didn't*** in speaking and informal writing.	The woman ***didn't* see** the train coming.
5. Time markers usually come at the beginning or end of a sentence.	
• Use ***ago*** after a length of time.	I started volunteering **a month *ago***. **A month *ago***, I started volunteering.
• Use ***last*** before words like *night*, *week*, or *year*.	I saw an accident ***last* night**.
• Use ***in*** with months, seasons, and years.	***In* 2011**, he became a real-life superhero.
• Use ***on*** with dates, and ***at*** with times.	The crime happened ***on*** May 23 ***at*** 11:00.
6. Questions in the simple past have the same form for regular and irregular verbs.	
• *Yes/No* questions follow the form: ***Did*** + **subject** + **base verb**	***Did* he save** the man? Yes, he did. Did you see him jump? No, I didn't.
• Most *Wh-* questions in the past begin with the question word followed by ***did*** + **subject** + **base verb**.	What ***did* you do**? I covered my eyes.
• Questions with *be* are formed by putting ***was*** or ***were*** before the subject.	***Were*** you surprised? Yes, I was.

2 Work with a partner. Look at the timeline of events in Wesley Autrey's life. Take turns asking and answering questions about the events.

Example

A: When was Wesley Autrey born?

B: He was born on February 6, 1956.

February 6, 1956   1968   1973   1977

• is born in Florida   • moves to New York   • joins the U.S. Navy   • leaves the Navy
                                                                      • becomes a
                                                                        construction worker

January 2, 2007 – 12:45   January 3   January 4

• sees Cameron Hollopeter   • gets many invitations   • New York City mayor
  fall on the train tracks   to speak in interviews   gives him the city's
• makes a quick decision to   and on TV   highest award
  jump down
• holds him down under the
  train
• hears people cheering
  from the platform

January 23, 2007   December 2007   2012

• goes to Washington D.C.   • wins the "Everyday Hero" • does another interview
• meets the president of   Award   • still doesn't think
  the United States   of himself as a hero

■■ GO TO MyEnglishLab FOR MORE GRAMMAR PRACTICE.

PRONUNCIATION

Sometimes the –ed ending is pronounced as a new syllable. Sometimes it is pronounced as a single sound at the end of the verb. Listen to the underlined words in the text.

🎧 Super Hero <u>trained</u> as a police officer and then <u>worked</u> as a professional wrestler. He <u>wanted</u> to make a difference in his community, so he <u>decided</u> to join the Real Life Hero Project. He <u>helped</u> to start Team Justice, Inc., a group that helps people in the community.

Write the verbs from the text on the correct lines.

The –ed ending is pronounced as a syllable:

_____

The –ed ending is pronounced as a single, final sound:

_____

RULES FOR PRONOUNCING THE -*ED* ENDING

The -*ed* ending is a syllable when the verb ends in a /t/ or /d/ sound. The -*ed* ending is pronounced /ɪd/ or /əd/.	decide–decid<u>ed</u> want–want<u>ed</u>	
The -*ed* ending is a final sound, /t/, when the verb ends in a voiceless sound.	work—work<u>ed</u> /k/ /kt/ miss—miss<u>ed</u> /s/ /st/	help—help<u>ed</u> /p/ /pt/ laugh—laugh<u>ed</u> /f/ /ft/
The -*ed* ending is a final sound, /d/, when the verb ends in a vowel sound or a voiced sound.	try—tri<u>ed</u> /ai/ /d/	train—train<u>ed</u> /n/ /nd/

1 🎧 Listen to the past tense verbs. Write the verbs in the correct column. Check your answers with a partner's and practice saying the verbs aloud.

arrived	inspired	pushed	thanked
carried	jumped	reacted	turned out
contributed	passed	saved	visited
covered	praised	showed	waited

-*ed* = /ɪd/ or /əd/   **-*ed* = /t/**   **-*ed* =/d/**

_____   _____   _____

_____   _____   _____

_____   _____   _____

_____   _____   _____

     _____

     _____

     _____

     _____

2 Work with a partner. Complete the sentences with the correct past tense verbs from the box in Exercise 1. Not all of the words will be used. Then, put the sentences in the correct order to tell Wesley Autrey's story. Practice telling the story to your partner.

_____ Luckily, everything _____ OK.

_____ It _____ over the top of the two men.

_____ Then, he _____ Mr. Hollopeter into the space between the tracks.

__1__ Wesley Autrey _____ quickly when he saw Cameron Hollopeter fall onto the subway tracks.

_____ He _____ for the train.

_____ The train _____ six seconds later.

_____ Later that day, Cameron Hollopeter's parents _____ him for saving their son's life.

_____ Two days later, the mayor of New York City _____ Wesley Autrey for his brave actions.

_____ First, he _____ down on to the tracks.

_____ He _____ Cameron Hollopeter's body and held him down.

SPEAKING SKILL

USING SIGNAL PHRASES IN PRESENTATIONS

We use signal phrases in presentations to introduce the topic and to signal a new idea or supporting detail. Signal phrases help the audience to understand your organization and follow your ideas.

Introducing Your Presentation	
• At the beginning of your presentation, you can get your audience's attention by	
• asking a question or	*How many of you have a hero?* *What do you think the word* hero *means?*
• making a general statement.	*Every year, many crimes happen in our city.* *There are many ways to define a hero.*
• Then, you can introduce your topic	*Today, I'd like to talk about . . .* *My topic today is . . .*

(continued on next page)

Making Transitions

There are different kinds of signal phrases you can use to introduce points, transition from one point to another, or give examples.	
• Introduce points	*Let me start with . . .* *First, I'd like to tell you . . .* *First of all,*
• Transition to a new point	*Next, I want to tell you . . .* *Now,* *Why is she my hero?*
• List points	*One reason/factor is . . .* *Another reason is . . .* *A final reason is . . .*
• Give examples	*For example, . . .* *Let me give you an example . . .*

Concluding Your Presentation

You can end your presentation by using a concluding phrase. A good concluding phrase helps your audience to remember your presentation.	*So, now you can see . . .* *This is why I think . . .* *I hope that you . . .*

Look at the presentation introduction and outline. Fill in the blanks with appropriate signal words and phrases. Practice saying the presentation with a partner.

My Hero: Pushpa Basnet

I. *Introduction: The person I admire*
    - *Pushpa Basnet*
    - *Young woman from Nepal*

    - Attention-getter: _____

    - Introduction: _____

    _____

    Transition to Part II: _____

II. *Background of Pushpa*

    - *Born in Kathmandu, Nepal*
    - *Studied social work in college*
    - *2005: 21 years old; started a daycare for children living in prison with their parents*
    - *2007: opened a home for children*
    - *2009: began a program to help parents in prison earn money for their children*
    - *2012: Won CNN Hero of the Year award*

    Transition to Part III. _____

III.   *Why I admire her*

Transition to Reason A _____

A.   *Has a good heart*
- *Gives the children a good home, food, clothing, and education*
- *Treats the prisoner's children like her own (e.g., lives with the children and they call her "Mommy")*

Transition to Reason B _____

B.   *Brave*
- *People said she couldn't do it (too young, not enough money)*
- *Had courage to do it; encouraged people to contribute money*

Transition to Reason C _____

C.   *Hardworking*
- *Works hard to get money for her programs*
- *Started programs by herself*
- *Manages the programs*
- *Takes care of the children*

IV.   *Concluding statement*

_____

■■■■■■■■■■■■■■■■■■■■■ *GO TO* MyEnglishLab *FOR MORE SKILL PRACTICE AND TO CHECK WHAT YOU LEARNED.*

FINAL SPEAKING TASK

In this activity, you will prepare a 2–3 minute presentation about someone you admire and present it to the class. You will introduce the person and explain why you admire this person. Try to use the vocabulary, grammar, pronunciation, and language for organizing a presentation that you learned in this unit.*

Follow the steps.

STEP 1: **Think of a topic.** Think of someone that you admire. It can be someone you know, or it can be someone famous that you know about.

*For Alternative Speaking Topics, see page 141.

STEP 2: Plan your Presentation. Complete the chart by researching and taking notes about the person. Be sure to list at least three reasons you admire this person and include details and examples. See the outline in Speaking Skills as an example.

WHO DO YOU ADMIRE?	NAME:
What is this person's background? Describe the person. Include information about things like the person's: • family background • job • volunteer work	Background:
Why do you admire this person? List at least three reasons and give details and examples.	Reason: Details/Example(s): Reason: Details/Example(s): Reason: Details/Example(s):

STEP 3: Make an outline. Write your outline on a separate piece of paper.

STEP 4: Practice your presentation with a partner. Use your outline and include signal phrases to introduce your topic, make transitions, and make a concluding statement. Get feedback from your partner.

STEP 5: Deliver your presentation to the class. Your classmates will listen, take notes, and ask you questions when you are finished.

Listening Task

Listen to the other students' presentations. Take notes. When you are finished, discuss these questions:

Which person is the most generous?

Which person is the bravest?

Which person is the best role model?

UNIT PROJECT

STEP 1: In this activity, you will research an organization that tries to help others in your community. Think about a problem in your community that you think needs to solved, such as homelessness, hunger, not enough education or jobs, or pollution.

STEP 2: Go on the Internet or ask people in your community to find an organization that is trying to solve this problem.

    a. What is the name of the organization?

    b. How many people volunteer or work for this organization?

    c. What do the volunteers do to help others? Give examples.

    d. Would you like to join this group? Why or why not?

STEP 3: Present your results to the class. Discuss which organization you would like to join.

ALTERNATIVE SPEAKING TOPICS

Work in a small group. Read and discuss the quotes. What do they mean to you? Explain each quote in your own words. Do you agree or disagree with the quote? Explain.

1. "You must be the change you want to see in the world."—Mahatma Gandhi
   Mahatma Gandhi (October 2, 1869–January 30, 1948) was an Indian leader who led the Indian people to independence from Britain.

2. "From what we get in life, we make a living. From what we give, we make a life."—Arthur Ashe
   Arthur Ashe (July 10, 1943–February 6, 1993) was the first African American to become the world's number one tennis player.

3. "The world is a dangerous place, not because of those who do bad things, but because of those who look on and do nothing."—Albert Einstein
   Albert Einstein (March 14, 1879–April 18, 1955) was a German-born theoretical physicist.

4. "Work for something because it is good, not just because it stands a chance to succeed."—Václav Havel
   Václav Havel (October 5, 1936–December 18, 2011) was a Czech writer and politician.

5. "And the trouble is, if you don't risk anything, you risk even more."—Erica Jong
   Erica Jong (born March 26, 1942) is an American author and teacher.

6. "I'd rather die for speaking out than to live and be silent."—Confucius
   Confucius (551–479 BCE) was a Chinese teacher, politician, and philosopher.

■■■■■■■■■■■■■■■■■■■■■■■■■■■ GO TO MyEnglishLab TO DISCUSS ONE OF THE ALTERNATIVE TOPICS, WATCH A VIDEO ABOUT HEROES, AND TAKE THE UNIT 6 ACHIEVEMENT TEST. ■■■■■■■■■■■■■■■■

GAMING YOUR WAY TO BETTER
Health

1 FOCUS ON THE TOPIC

1. Look at the photo. What are the people doing?

2. Read the title of the unit. Do you think that video games can help us to improve our health? What are some negative effects of video games on our health?

3. *Technology* means new kinds of machines or ways of doing things using science and knowledge. What are some ways that technology can help us to stay healthy?

GO TO MyEnglishLab TO CHECK WHAT YOU KNOW.

VOCABULARY

1 🎧 Read and listen to the website about a serious disease: diabetes.

SOME FREQUENTLY ASKED QUESTIONS (FAQS) ABOUT DIABETES

HOME

Diabetes is a very serious public health problem in the United States today. Here are some important facts about this **illness**.

CONTACT

What is diabetes?
In diabetics, too much sugar collects in the blood. This can lead to very serious health problems.

ABOUT US

How serious is the problem?
In the United States, diabetes affects one out of 10 adults, and one out of 400 children.

How does diabetes affect everyday life?
- *Careful control of sugar:* Diabetics have to carefully control how much sugar they eat. This is an important part of the **treatment** for diabetes. However, it can be very hard for children to stay away from sugary foods and drinks.

- *Blood sugar level tests:* To check their blood sugar levels, diabetics must test their blood several times a day. They do this by pricking a finger with a small **needle**. Children with diabetes find it especially hard to **follow instructions** and do what the doctor says. After all, most children hate needles, so they don't have the **motivation** to take care of their health.

- *Exercise:* **Physical** exercise is very important for diabetics. As we all know, young people today spend a lot of time indoors, sitting in front of a television or computer screen rather than running around and playing. In fact, there is a **connection** between not getting exercise and developing diabetes. Exercise helps patients control their blood sugar, and people who don't exercise are more likely to develop this disease.

- *How can doctors **motivate** diabetic **patients** to follow their instructions?* Are rewards the answer, for example, giving patients special prizes for making healthy choices? Some leaders in healthcare think so. They are working with computer game designers to make games that will help patients take care of their health.

- *Are games and rewards really the answer?* Other healthcare leaders do not believe that games are a serious solution. They think that games just **put a Band-Aid® on** the problem. According to them, the problem is that we are a society of **couch potatoes**. We spend too much time indoors, eating junk food and not getting enough exercise. They **criticize** video games, saying they are a part of the problem, not the solution. They believe that dealing with illnesses such as diabetes will take deeper changes in society. These include changes in eating habits and levels of physical activity.

---

2 Match the words on the left with the definitions on the right.

_____ **1.** needle

_____ **2.** follow instructions

_____ **3.** treatment

_____ **4.** physical

_____ **5.** connection

_____ **6.** patient

_____ **7.** motivation

_____ **8.** motivate (someone)

_____ **9.** put a Band-Aid on

_____ **10.** couch potato

_____ **11.** criticize

_____ **12.** illness

a. someone who spends a lot of time sitting, usually watching television

b. interest in and willingness to do something without needing to be told or forced to do it

c. a sickness

d. create a solution that is temporary and won't solve a problem

e. to talk about the problems or faults of someone or something

f. something that is done to help someone who is injured or ill

g. having to do with our bodies

h. to do something in the way someone has told you to do it

i. a very thin pointed steel tube that is pushed through the skin to put a drug into the body or to take blood out

j. someone who is getting help from a doctor or is in a hospital

k. relationship; the way in which two facts, ideas, events, etc. are related to each other, and one is affected or caused by the other

l. to give someone a reason for doing something

GO TO MyEnglishLab FOR MORE VOCABULARY PRACTICE.

PREVIEW

A hospital administrator (manager) is leading a meeting.

(headphones) Listen to the beginning of the meeting. Circle the letter of the correct answer to each question.

1. Who is the administrator talking to?

   a. patients

   b. doctors

   c. video game designers

2. What is the purpose of the meeting?

   a. to help doctors understand technology

   b. to teach doctors how to play video games

   c. to introduce doctors to video games that will help them and their patients

How do you think video games can help doctors and patients? List three ideas.

1. _____

2. _____

3. _____

MAIN IDEAS

1 (headphones) Listen to the complete meeting. Look again at your answers from the Preview section. Were any of your answers correct? Did your answers help you understand the meeting?

2 Circle the correct answers.

1. What is it sometimes difficult for doctors to get patients to do?

   a. to follow their instructions

   b. to stop playing video games

   c. to get rewards for being healthy

2. How might video games help patients?

    a. They might teach patients about their illnesses.

    b. They might motivate patients to stay healthy.

    c. They might help patients to have fun.

3. What types of games does the administrator mention?

    a. games for children

    b. games for adults

    c. games for children and adults

4. Which health problems can these games help with?

    a. diabetes and burns

    b. diabetes and cancer

    c. cancer and burns

5. Do the doctors agree that video games will be useful for their patients?

    a. Some do, but others are not sure.

    b. They disagree.

    c. They agree.

DETAILS

Listen again. Then read each statement. Write **T** *(true)* or **F** *(false)*. Then, correct the false statements.

_____ **1.** The doctors think that people who play video games are healthy and thin.

_____ **2.** Video games motivate people because they are fun.

_____ **3.** The first doctor, Sam, thinks video games will motivate patients to care about their health.

_____ **4.** In one game, the kid with diabetes is a superhero.

(continued on next page)

_____ **5.** In this game, patients get a reward for following their doctor's treatment plan.

_____ **6.** Children with diabetes don't mind checking their blood sugar.

_____ **7.** The doctors at the meeting treat mostly children, rather than adults.

_____ **8.** *Snow World* is a video game for children with diabetes.

_____ **9.** In *Snow World,* patients wear special glasses and earplugs.

_____ **10.** *Snow World* works because patients have more fun during treatment.

■■ GO TO MyEnglishLab FOR MORE LISTENING PRACTICE.

MAKE INFERENCES

PERSUASION

An inference is a guess about something that is not directly stated. To make an inference, use information that you understand from what you hear.

In this meeting, the administrator tries to *persuade* the doctors to agree with her. That is, she tries to get them to agree with her. To do this, she does two things. First, she shows that she understands why they may disagree. Then, she uses words and phrases that will get them to agree with her opinion.

🎧 Listen to the example. Listen for what the speaker says to show her understanding of why the doctors may disagree with her ideas. Then decide what the speaker's *intended meaning* is. That is, decide the true meaning of what the speaker is saying.

Example

I know that people criticize video games—and that we don't usually hear the words "video game" and "good health" together in one sentence. In fact, just the opposite, right?

What is the administrator's intended meaning?

a. Most people think video games are not good for health.

b. Most people think video games are good for health.

By saying "I know that people criticize video games," the administrator shows that she understands what listeners' opinion or attitude toward the subject is. She understands that many doctors have the opinion that video games are not good for our health.

Excerpt One

a. In the past she thought video games were always bad for children's health, but then she changed her mind.

b. She understands why children play video games, but she thinks they must stop spending so much time playing them.

How do you know? What key words does she use to show her intended meaning?

_____

Excerpt Two

a. She agrees with Sam.

b. She disagrees with Sam.

How do you know? What key words does she use to show her intended meaning?

_____

EXPRESS OPINIONS

Work with two other students. Answer the questions. Give reasons for your opinions.

1. Do you think that video games are a good way to motivate patients? Why or why not? Did the administrator persuade you to agree with her?

2. What are some other ways to motivate people to take care of their health?

3. Do you like to play video games? What are some advantages and disadvantages of playing video games?

■■■■■■■■■■■■■■■■■■■■■■■■ *GO TO* MyEnglishLab *TO GIVE YOUR OPINION ABOUT ANOTHER QUESTION.*

VOCABULARY

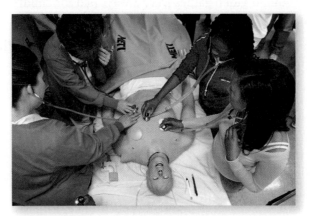

Medical students training with a dummy patient

Say the words in the box aloud. Then read the sentences and circle the letter of the answer that best explains the meaning of the boldfaced word.

| convinced | enthusiasm | simulation | support | traditional |

1. **A:** You can't just give your opinion. You need to **support** it with facts.

   B: But what if I don't have any facts?

   A: Then you need to do some research.

   a. find
   b. make it stronger

2. **A:** I'm not **convinced** that this treatment is the best way to deal with my son's illness.

   B: Why not? The doctor recommended it, didn't he?

   A: Yes, but I would like to talk to a few more doctors. I want more information before making such a big decision.

   a. happy
   b. sure

3. **A:** How do you like your new flight **simulation** video game?

   B: I love it! I really feel like I'm flying a real airplane.

   A: Sounds fun. I'll have to come over and try it out sometime.

   a. copying a situation that is similar to a real one
   b. making a game that is fun to play

4. **A:** My new students are great.

   B: What makes them so special?

   A: They have a lot of **enthusiasm** for medicine. They spend extra hours in the lab and always ask me a lot of good questions to learn more.

   a. excitement and interest

   b. knowledge

5. **A:** So how do you like our new teacher?

   B: He's OK, but his teaching is so **traditional**.

   A: What do you mean?

   B: Well, he's doesn't use any new teaching strategies or technology. I think he teaches us in the same way he learned when he was a kid.

   a. following old ideas and ways instead of new ones

   b. boring and not interesting

■■■■■■■■■■■■■■■■■■■■■■■■■■■■■■■■■■■■■ GO TO MyEnglishLab FOR MORE VOCABULARY PRACTICE.

COMPREHENSION

Listen to a conversation between two medical school professors. One is male and the other is female. Write **M** next to phrases that refer to the male professor and **F** next to phrases that refer to the female professor.

_____ **1.** is enthusiastic about his/her new students

_____ **2.** uses a reward system with his/her students

_____ **3.** is enthusiastic about the simulation lab

_____ **4.** knows about the research regarding simulations and medical training

_____ **5.** thinks that traditional ways of training doctors are better than the current ones

_____ **6.** might be open to changing his/her mind about technology and medical training

LISTENING SKILL

UNDERSTANDING DOUBT

In this meeting, the doctors hear about some new and unusual medical technology: video games and simulations. Some of them express *doubt* that this technology is a good idea. They aren't convinced that it will work well in healthcare. You can hear their attitudes in their words and intonation.

🎧 Listen to the example.

Example

> *Video games can help you motivate your patients to make the right choices, to follow your instructions, and to stay healthy. It's really that simple. Yes, Sam? You have a question?*
>
> *Hmmm . . . I don't know about this. I mean, I know it's sometimes hard to get patients to do what's best for their health, but I'm not sure games are the answer. Isn't that just putting a Band-Aid on a much deeper problem?*

In this example, the doctor expresses his doubt when he says *Hmmm . . . I don't know about this . . .* He uses a flat intonation to mean that he isn't convinced video games are a good idea.

Here are some expressions that are used to express doubt:

Hmmm . . . /Well/Yeah . . . (with flat intonation)	I don't know . . .
Maybe, but . . .	Do you really think . . . ?
I can see . . . but . . .	Are you sure?

🎧 Listen to the excerpts. How does the speaker express doubt? Then circle the letter of the statement that shows the second speaker's intended meaning.

Excerpt One

What expression does the speaker use to express doubt?

_____

What is her intended meaning?

a. I am not convinced that video games will work with kids.

b. I am not convinced that video games will work with adults.

Excerpt Two

What two expressions does the second speaker use to show doubt?

_____

_____

What is his intended meaning?

a. I am not convinced your students are learning anything.

b. I am not convinced your students can learn communication skills

■■■■■■■■■■■■■■■■■■■■■■■■■■■■■■■■■■■ GO TO MyEnglishLab FOR MORE SKILL PRACTICE.

STEP 1: Organize

Complete the chart with details from Listenings One and Two.

VIDEO GAMES IN HEALTHCARE	ADVANTAGES	DISADVANTAGES
LISTENING 1: FOR PATIENTS	Motivate patients to _____ Examples: – _Diabetics_ _____ – _____	Too much time _indoors_ _____ Not enough _____
LISTENING 2: FOR MEDICAL STUDENTS	_Enthusiasm_ _____ _____	Not doing _____ Not practicing on _____

STEP 2: Synthesize

Work with a partner. Student A, you are enthusiastic about the use of video games to help people live healthier lives and train medical students. Student B, you are uncertain about these uses of video games. Use the information from the notes you completed in Step 1: Organize.

Example

A: Video games are a good idea. If kids have serious illnesses, they can learn to follow their doctors' instructions.

B: I'm not so sure about that. Don't you think children spend enough time in front of computer screens?

Now switch roles. Student A is now uncertain about the use of video games in helping people to get and stay healthy. Student B is now enthusiastic.

■■■■■■■■■■■■■■■■■■■■■■■■■■■■■■■■■ GO TO MyEnglishLab TO CHECK WHAT YOU LEARNED.

VOCABULARY

REVIEW

Use the words and expressions in the box to complete the conversation below. Then practice the conversation with a partner.

connected to	illness	physically
convinced	motivation	traditional
couch potato	patient	treatment

Conversation between two friends

A: You've been so helpful during my son's _____. I really appreciate
1.

everything you've done.

B: Oh please, there's no need to thank me. I know you'd do the same for me. It's the least

I could do. So what do the doctors say? How is the _____ going?
2.

A: It's going really well, in fact. The doctors say that Timmy is an excellent

_____. He's very good at following their instructions. He's
3.

doing everything they tell him to do. And it helps that he's never been a

_____. He's always been an active kid, even when he got so sick.
4.

B: It sounds like he's a strong kid—both _____ and emotionally.
5.

A: Yeah, his _____ is high—he really wants to get better. And everyone
6.

says that's the most important thing. The doctors say that his desire to get well

is strongly _____ the success of this treatment. He's always been
7.

_____ that he will be able to fight this thing and win. Also, the doctors
8.

are confident that this new treatment is much better than the _____
9.

way of treating his disease. So we are very hopeful.

4 APPS TO A HEALTHIER YOU

HOME

CONTACT

ABOUT US

Download these apps on your smartphone, and start getting healthy today!

1. *Start Walking Path*

This app was created by the American Heart Association to **encourage** people to walk more to **stay fit**. It makes it easy for you to find or create and then share nice walks wherever you are. For example, imagine you take a walk through a park on your way home from work one day. You can map your walk using this app and share it with your friends and coworkers so they can enjoy it too. Or you can search a new area to see if anyone else has **posted** a nice walk.

2. *Weigh What Matters*

This app was created by the American Medical Association to make it easy for patients to set healthy goals and then **keep track of** their **progress**. The app tracks three areas: weight, nutrition, and physical activity. Users record what they weigh, what they eat, and how much exercise they get. From this information, a progress report is created and emailed to the patient's doctor. If patients are not getting enough exercise, their doctors can encourage them to **work out** more often.

3. *MyFitnessPal*

This app allows you to easily keep track of everything you eat and shows you the calories you are consuming. You can also keep track of or find recipes for healthy meals. And it has links to discussion boards where you can **get support** from other people who are trying to lose weight.

4. *Sleep Cycle*

This app watches you while you sleep. It then teaches you about your sleep **patterns**. You can then use the information to change your patterns if necessary so that you can sleep better. Here's how it works. You place your phone on your bed, near your pillow. Then just go to sleep—your phone keeps track of your movement and breathing during the night. It records this information in an easy-to-read graph that shows you how much you move and how often and when you wake up during the night. It also chooses the best time to wake you up, so that you have a peaceful start to your day.

Write the boldfaced word or phrase from the web page next to the correct definition.

1. _____ to do exercise to improve your health or physical fitness

2. _____ the regular and repeated ways things happen or are done

3. _____ to stay physically healthy and strong

(continued on next page)

4. _____ to persuade someone to do something

5. _____ to get approval or help from someone

6. _____ pay attention to

7. _____ improvements over time

8. _____ put up so others can see it

CREATE

Work in a small group. Take turns asking and answering the questions. Use the boldfaced words and vocabulary from Review and Expand in your answers.

1. Are you **convinced** that using video games and simulations are effective for training doctors to deal with **patients**? Why or why not?

2. What do you think is the best **motivation** to take care of your health? In other words, why should people want to take care of their health? How can doctors **encourage** their patients to be healthy?

3. Do you like to **work out**, either in a gym or at home? If not, do you do any other sports or activities to **stay fit**? Do you **keep track of** your **progress**?

4. Do you keep a regular sleep **pattern**, or do you sleep at different times during the week?

5. Do you use any **traditional treatments** or medicines to take care of your health? If so, what do you use?

6. Do you think there is a **connection** between your feelings and your **physical** health? Give an example.

GO TO MyEnglishLab *FOR MORE VOCABULARY PRACTICE.*

GRAMMAR

1 Read the conversation. Notice the modals of advice that appear in bold.

A: I **should** go for a walk after dinner. Do you want to come with me?

B: Great idea! My doctor said I **ought to** get more exercise.

A: My too-tight pants are telling me I **ought to** get more exercise!

MODALS OF ADVICE AND NECESSITY: *SHOULD / OUGHT TO / HAVE TO*

1. Use *should* to give advice or talk about what is right to do. Use *should* + the base form of the verb.	She should **follow** her doctor's instructions. NOT: She should ~~to follow~~ her doctor's instructions. NOT: She should ~~follows~~ her doctor's instructions.
Use *should not* for the negative.	Diabetics **should not** eat too much sugar.
Use the contraction *shouldn't* in speaking and informal writing.	Diabetics **shouldn't** eat too much sugar.
2. We use *should* to talk about the present or future.	You **should** call the doctor **now**. You **should** go to the doctor **tomorrow**.
Ought to means the same as *should*. *Ought to* is not usually used in questions or negatives. We use *should* instead.	We **ought** to exercise more. **Should** I join a health club? NOT: ~~Ought I to join~~ a health club? NOT: I ~~ought not to play~~ so many video games. I think you **should** exercise more. Maybe you **ought to** spend less time playing video games.
3. Use **have to** or **has to** to talk about things that are necessary. Use *have/has to* + the base form of the verb.	I **have to** take medicine every day. She **has to** lose weight.
Use *don't* or *doesn't have to* to talk about things that are not necessary.	I **don't have to** go to the doctor today. He **doesn't have to** lose weight.
4. To make questions with *have to*, use *do/does* + subject + *have to* + the base form of the verb.	**Do you have to** go to the doctor today? **Does he have to** keep track of what he eats?
5. We use *have/has to* to talk about the present or future.	I **have to** check my blood sugar **right now**. He **has to** go to the doctor **tomorrow**.

2 Complete the conversation with the correct modal verbs. Use *should/shouldn't; ought to; have/has to; don't/doesn't have to.* In some cases, more than one modal verb might be correct.

A: Hi. How are you?

B: Oh, not great. I'm so tired. I was up all night studying, and now I have soccer practice.

A: Oh, that's too bad. Maybe you _____ go to practice today.
1.

B: That's a good idea, but I _____ go because we have a game tomorrow.
2.

Everyone needs me there.

A: I know! You _____ try one of those energy drinks. I hear they can
3.

really wake you up.

B: Really? _____ I really have an energy drink[1] before I exercise? I'm not
4.

sure that's a good idea.

A: Why not? Energy drinks are full of vitamins. And I heard that they can help you play

better. A lot of athletes use them these days.

B: Well, I heard a news report about those energy drinks. It said that many of them are

unhealthy. They have a lot of caffeine and sugar, and you really _____
5.

drink them before you exercise.

A: Wow, I didn't know that. Then I think you _____ try the most natural
6.

thing.

B: Really? What's that?

A: Sleep!

3 🎧 Listen to the conversation and check your answers.

---

[1] **energy drink:** a drink that gives you the ability to be active and do a lot without feeling tired

4 Work in a group of three. Write a health or food problem that you (or a friend) have. Tell the group the problem. The other members of your group will give you advice. Use *should/ought to* and *have to*.

Example

STUDENT A: I fall asleep right away, but then I wake up an hour later and can't get back to sleep.

STUDENT B: I think you ought to try to exercise every day—but early in the day. That way you'll be more tired at night.

STUDENT C: I think you should drink a glass of hot milk before bed. That usually works for me.

The problem:

_____

_____

Advice:

_____

_____

GO TO MyEnglishLab *FOR MORE GRAMMAR PRACTICE.*

PRONUNCIATION

REDUCTIONS

In speaking, the modal verbs *ought to, have to,* and *has to* are often reduced. That is, they are pronounced as one word, not two words, and they are not stressed. Usually, the main verb is stressed.

Have to *Have to* is pronounced as one word, /hæftə/. The letter *v* is pronounced /f/. The vowel in *to* is usually pronounced /ə/.	Do you have to /hæftə/ take your medicine? I have to /hæftə/ sleep more.
Has to *Has to* is pronounced as one word, /hæstə/. The vowel in *to* is usually pronounced /ə/.	He has to /hæstə/ quit smoking.
Ought to *Ought to* is pronounced as one word, /ɒdə/.* The vowel in *ought to* sounds like the vowel in *father*. The vowel in *to* is usually pronounced /ə/. The consonant *t* is usually changed to a fast "d" sound: /ɒdə/. *In some dialects of English, the vowel in *ought* is pronounced /ɔ/. This vowel is like the vowel in *saw*.	He ought to /ɒdə/ exercise.

1 🎧 Listen to the conversations and fill in the missing words. You might need to write more than one word in the blank.

Conversation 1

A: I'm worried about you. You _____ play so many video games. You

1.

really _____ spend more time outdoors.

2.

B: Yeah, I know I _____ exercise more, but I'm so tired all the time.

3.

A: Well, maybe you aren't getting enough sleep. You _____ get one of

4.

those sleep apps. You know, for your phone?

B: How much do I _____ pay for that?

5.

A: You _____ pay a cent. It's free.

6.

B: Really? That sounds great.

A: Yeah, you _____ go online and check it out.

7.

A: What do you think? _____ I buy a smartphone for my son?
1.

B: Yes! You _____ get him one! I know you're worried about his health—
2.

a smartphone is a great idea.

A: I'm sorry, but I'm afraid I don't see the connection between cell phones and health.

B: Well . . . there are so many great apps he can download that will motivate him to

exercise and eat right.

A: That's crazy! Are you telling me he _____ have a cell phone to get
3.

healthy?

B: No, he _____ have one, but it really can help.
4.

A: How?

B: Well, for example, there's an app called MyFitnessPal. He can use it to record what he

eats every day. It gives information about things like nutrition and calories.

A: Oh, come on! He can keep track of his calories now. I _____ buy him a
5.

fancy cell phone for that.

B: You know, you _____ at least check it out before you criticize it.
6.

2 🎧 Listen to the conversations in Exercise 1 again. Listen carefully to the reductions.
Then practice the conversations with a partner. Try to use reductions.

SPEAKING SKILL

EXPRESSING CONCERN, GIVING AND RECEIVING ADVICE

When someone has a problem, it's polite to express concern. Sometimes we also want to offer some advice. When we give advice to someone else, it is polite to use *maybe* with *should* or *ought to*, or to use another polite expression.

Expressing Concern	Giving Polite Advice	Receiving Advice
What's the matter?	*Maybe you should* . . . change your sleep patterns.	That's a good idea.
What's wrong?	*Maybe you ought to* . . . go to the doctor.	Thanks for the advice.
That's too bad.	*You might want to* . . . get some rest.	I'll give it a try.
I'm sorry to hear that.	*Why don't you try* having some hot tea?	Thanks anyway, but I'd rather . . .
	Have you tried . . . exercising?	

1 Work with a partner. Look at the chart with health problems and ways to prevent (stop) or treat them. Think of two more ways to prevent each problem and add them to the chart.

HEALTH PROBLEM	WAYS TO PREVENT OR TREAT IT
HEART DISEASE	• do not eat a lot of red meat • •
DIABETES	• exercise • •
INSOMNIA (NOT BEING ABLE TO SLEEP)	• drink a glass of warm milk before bed • •
STRESS	• listen to relaxing music • •
HEADACHES	• get at least 8 hours of sleep a night • •

2 Walk around the classroom and talk to five other students. Practice expressing concern and giving advice.

Example

A: What's the matter?

B: I have insomnia.

A: I'm sorry to hear that. Why don't you try drinking a glass of warm milk before bed?

B: Thanks for the advice. I'll give it a try.

■■■■■■■■■■■■■■■■■ GO TO MyEnglishLab FOR MORE SKILL PRACTICE AND TO CHECK WHAT YOU LEARNED.

FINAL SPEAKING TASK

In this activity, you will prepare and present a television commercial for a video game or an application for a smartphone that will help people get and stay healthy. Try to use the grammar, pronunciation, vocabulary, and language for expressing concern and giving and receiving advice that you learned in this unit.* Work in groups of three.

Follow the steps.

STEP 1: Decide on a video game or a smartphone application (app) that will help people get and stay healthy. You can use one of the following ideas, or think of your own idea.

A video game or app to:

- help people stop smoking

- help people develop healthier sleep patterns

- help people lose weight

- help people eat healthier food

- help people to become more physically active

- help medical students learn how to be more understanding of their patients

- help people manage stress

---

*For Alternative Speaking Topics, see page 165.

STEP 2: Design a television commercial to introduce your game or app to the public. Include the following information in your commercial:

- a conversation between someone who has the problem that the game or app is designed to address and someone who is using it. The person who is using it should give advice to the person who has the problem

- a description of what it is and how it works

- a description of who it is designed for (for example, teenagers, young adults, etc.)

STEP 3: Present your commercial to the class.

Listening Task

As you listen to your classmates present their commercials, fill in the chart.

TOPIC OF THE COMMERCIAL	AUDIENCE	ADVICE	WAS THE COMMERCIAL EFFECTIVE? WHY OR WHY NOT?
1.			
2.			
3.			
4.			

UNIT PROJECT

STEP 1: Find out more about technology that can be used by doctors or ordinary people to help people lead healthier lives. Choose one topic from the list.

- Robots that operate on patients
- Video games that encourage people to take better care of their teeth
- Video games like *Snow World* that help patients manage their pain
- Virtual reality games that are used to train doctors
- Cell phone applications that encourage people to stop unhealthy behavior such as drinking too much alcohol, smoking, eating junk food, or not getting enough exercise

STEP 2: Research the topic on the Internet or in the library.

STEP 3: Share your information with the class. Include the following information:

- Who is the technology designed for?
- What does it do?
- How does it work?
- Is it effective? Are there any studies that show how well it works?

ALTERNATIVE SPEAKING TOPICS

Work in a small group. Read the quotes about health. Explain each quote in your own words. Discuss whether you follow the advice or not.

"An apple a day keeps the doctor away."—Author unknown

"Every human being is the author of his own health or disease."—Siddhartha Gautama

"To lengthen thy life, lessen thy meals."—Benjamin Franklin

"True silence is the rest of the mind and is to the spirit what sleep is to the body, nourishment and refreshment."—William Penn

"Those who think they have not time for bodily exercise will sooner or later have to find time for illness."—Edward Stanley

"A wise man should consider that health is the greatest of human blessings and learn how by his own thought to derive benefit from his illnesses."—Hippocrates

■■■■■■■■■■■■■■■■■■■■■■■■■■■ *GO TO* MyEnglishLab *TO DISCUSS ONE OF THE ALTERNATIVE TOPICS, WATCH A VIDEO ABOUT HEALTH PROBLEMS, AND TAKE THE UNIT 7 ACHIEVEMENT TEST.* ■■■■■■■■■■■■■■

ENDANGERED
Languages

1 FOCUS ON THE TOPIC

1. What do you think the people are talking about? What language do you think they are speaking?

2. What do you think an endangered language is? Why do you think people stop speaking a language?

3. Do you speak the same language as your parents? As your grandparents? Why or why not?

GO TO MyEnglishLab TO CHECK WHAT YOU KNOW.

LISTENING ONE | **LANGUAGE LOSS**

VOCABULARY

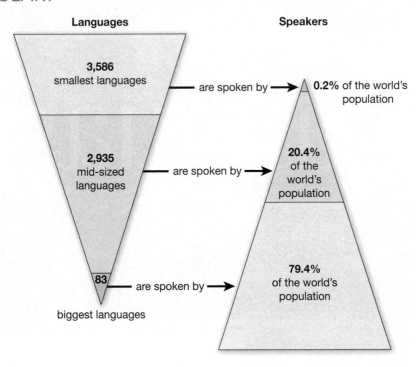

1 🎧 Read and listen to an excerpt from a textbook about endangered languages.

LANGUAGE TODAY

DISAPPEARING LANGUAGES

1   There are more than 6,000 languages in the world today. Unfortunately, many of these languages are **endangered**. An endangered language is a language that few people are learning to speak. When an endangered language loses all of its speakers, it becomes **extinct**. Sometimes a language **disappears** when the language of a more powerful or **dominant** community **replaces** it. For example, this happened when English replaced many native languages in North America. Today, many Native Americans only speak English instead of the native language of their culture.

2   Many **linguists** study endangered languages and work to **preserve** them. A number of speakers of these languages also work hard to save them for

future generations. In many communities, there are special programs that teach children their **native language**. These programs are important for children to **acquire** their native language. The children in these programs grow up to be **bilingual**—they can speak two languages; the language of the more powerful community, as well as their native language.

2 Choose the best synonym or definition for each word or phrase.

1. **endangered**

   a. might die soon   **b.** already dead

2. **extinct**

   a. no longer existing   **b.** very old

3. **disappears**

   a. stops being useful   **b.** stops being used

4. **dominant**

   a. strong   **b.** easy to learn

5. **replaces**

   a. changes for something else   **b.** stops

6. **linguists**

   a. people who speak the same language   **b.** people who study the science of language

7. **preserve**

   a. save   **b.** lose

8. **native language**

   a. a language only old people speak   **b.** a language that belongs to the place of one's birth

9. **bilingual**

   a. speaking one language   **b.** speaking two languages

10. **acquire**

   a. learn   **b.** speak

GO TO MyEnglishLab TO CHECK WHAT YOU KNOW.

PREVIEW

Listen to the beginning of a lecture on language loss. Read and answer each question.

1. Where is the speaker?

   a. in a class

   b. on TV

   c. on the radio

2. What is the topic?

   a. endangered languages

   b. endangered languages and cultures

   c. endangered and dead languages

3. What do you think the speaker will talk about? Make three predictions.

   _____

   _____

   _____

MAIN IDEAS

1. Listen to the whole lecture. Then look again at your predictions from the Preview section. Were your predictions correct? Did they help you understand the lecture?

2. Read each statement. Write **T** (true) or **F** (false).

   _____ 1. Linguists care about endangered languages because, when a language dies, a culture can die, too.

   _____ 2. Languages become endangered when children don't go to school.

   _____ 3. Sometimes the government makes it illegal to speak a language.

   _____ 4. Dominant communities usually learn the language of the less powerful community.

   _____ 5. Linguists try to save endangered languages.

DETELS

Listen to the lecture again. Then circle the best answer to complete each statement.

1. By the year 2100, _____ of the world's languages could be extinct.

   a. 50 percent   **b.** 40 percent   **c.** 20 percent

2. The Manx people lost their native _____.

   a. culture   **b.** traditions   **c.** language

3. According to the speaker, _____ may be lost when a language disappears.

   a. books, schools, and teachers   **b.** culture, history, and knowledge   **c.** customs, communities and way of life

4. Before 1987, it was _____ to teach Hawaiian in public schools.

   a. illegal   **b.** required   **c.** difficult

5. Today, more than _____ students are enrolled in Hawaiian language programs.

   a. 1,000   **b.** 2,000   **c.** 12,000

6. Once there were _____ Native American languages, but now many have become extinct.

   a. several   **b.** hundreds of   **c.** thousands of

7. In Greenland, students learn _____.

   a. Kalaallisut and Danish   **b.** only Danish   **c.** only Kalaallisut

8. Linguists help create _____ programs where people can study endangered languages.

   a. interesting   **b.** community   **c.** unusual

9. Linguists preserve languages by _____.

   a. recording them, studying them, and by writing story books   **b.** studying them, learning them, and writing history books   **c.** recording them, studying them, and writing grammar books

■■■■■■■■■■■■■■■■■■■■■■■■■■■■■■■■■■ GO TO MyEnglishLab FOR MORE LISTENING PRACTICE.

MAKE INFERENCES

SPEAKER'S VIEWPOINT

An inference is a guess about something that is not directly stated. To make an inference, use information that you understand from what you hear.

A speaker's viewpoint is the speaker's opinion on a subject. Knowing a speaker's viewpoint will help you understand the points made. The speaker's viewpoint is not always stated clearly. You may need to guess or infer the viewpoint.

(◌) Listen to the example. Then read the statement. What is the speaker's viewpoint?

Example

PROFESSOR: Good morning, everybody. Today, I'd like to talk about endangered and dead languages. So . . . who did the reading for today? Hmm . . . I see . . . some of you did . . . Then, who can tell me what a dead language is?

The professor says, "I see some of you did." The professor wants all the students to do the reading and be prepared to discuss. You can infer that he probably would agree that many students are not prepared for class.

(◌) Listen to two excerpts from the lecture. After listening to each excerpt, answer the questions. Discuss your answers with the class.

Excerpt One

Do you think the professor would agree or disagree with the statement: "Language programs are a good way to preserve languages."

a. agree   **b.** disagree

Excerpt Two

Do you think the student would agree or disagree with the following statement: "I'm not sure it's worth it to preserve languages."?

a. agree   **b.** disagree

EXPRESS OPINIONS

Work in a small group. Read the different opinions about language. Then say whether you agree or disagree with the opinions and explain why.

Language is a very important part of one's culture. That's why we should preserve languages.

I think each country should have only one official language. People who live in the same country should speak the same language.

I think it's important for people to learn more than one language. That way they can understand different people and cultures.

■■■■■■■■■■■■■■■■■■■■■■■■■ *GO TO* MyEnglishLab *TO GIVE YOUR OPINION ABOUT ANOTHER QUESTION.*

VOCABULARY

1 Read the blog entry. Pay attention to the boldfaced words.

LANGUAGE LOSS STUDY

HOME

CONTACT

ABOUT US

1   If you follow my blog, you know I travel all over the world studying endangered languages. It is very interesting learning about languages and cultures. I have posted some stories of people I recently met. The stories are about a language that once was the (1) **official language** of a country. Everyone spoke the language. But things changed, and it was no longer the official language. As you know, when this happens, a language can become extinct. This is exactly what people were worried about. So, a group of people (2) **got together** to tell me their stories and to talk about doing something about the situation. They (3) **came up with** some great ideas, some ways to help slow the loss of their language. They had to work with the government on their (4) **policy**. They created some rules about language teaching. Without people like this, languages will (5) **eventually** become extinct.

2   I hope you'll enjoy listening to some of my stories. I think they are really interesting!

2 Match the boldfaced words with their definitions. Write the number of the words.

_____ **a.** a rule or plan

_____ **b.** in the end

_____ **c.** created, thought about

_____ **d.** met

_____ **e.** the main language used in a country

■■■ GO TO MyEnglishLab FOR MORE VOCABULARY PRACTICE.

COMPREHENSION

Listen to the speaker talk about her experience with her native language and culture. Then read each question and circle the correct answer.

1. Where does she live?

    a. New Zealand   b. Greenland

2. What language did she learn in school?

    a. Maori   b. English

3. What language did her grandparents speak?

    a. Maori   b. English

4. How did she feel in her family?

    a. empty and different   b. happy and excited

5. Where do her children learn Maori language and culture?

    a. in elementary school   b. in language nests

6. What is a language nest?

    a. a pre-school   b. a home school

7. How many language nests are there now?

    a. a few hundred   b. over 400

8. What are three Maori values that children learn?

    a. love, caring, and respect for elders   b. hope, sharing, and family responsibilities

9. Who teaches the Maori adults their language and culture?

    a. linguists   b. older Maoris

10. Where do they meet?

    a. in schools   b. in neighborhood centers

11. What is/are the official language(s) of New Zealand now?

    a. English   b. English and Maori

LISTENING SKILL

LISTENING FOR REASONS AND EXAMPLES

Identifying reasons and examples that support the main idea can help you understand the main idea. Some words and phrases that identify reasons are: *the reason . . . , this is because . . . ,* and *that's why . . .* Some words and phrases that identify and list examples are: *for example . . . , an example of this is . . . , also . . . , for instance . . . ,* and *another . . .*

🎧 Listen to the examples:

Example 1

In school, I learned and spoke English. This is because English was the official language. Everything was taught in English in school. That was the government policy.

Main idea   In school, I learned and spoke English.

Reason   This is because English was the official language.

Reason   That was the government policy.

The main idea is that English was the only language she learned and used in school. The reason is English was the official language and it was the government policy. She says, "This is because English was the official language."

Example 2

Through the language nests, children learn about the values and traditions of the Maori culture. For example, we have a strong belief in love, compassion, caring, hospitality, family responsibilities, and respect for elders. Also, children learn our Maori stories, which are a big part of our tradition.

Main idea   Through the language nests, children learn about Maori traditions and the basic values of the Maori culture.

Example   For example, we have a strong belief in love, compassion, caring, hospitality, family responsibilities, and respect for elders.

Example   Also, children learn our Maori stories, which are a big part of our tradition.

The main idea is the children learn the values and traditions of Maori culture. Examples of values are a strong belief in love, compassion, caring, hospitality, family responsibilities and respect for elders. Another example is children learn about Maori stories, which are part of their tradition.

🎧 Listen to the excerpts. Write the missing words to complete the main idea and the word or phrase that introduces each statement to support the main idea. Then, decide if each statement is a reason or an example. Circle the correct answer.

Excerpt One

Main Idea: We are also trying _____.

_____, I now attend classes that meet in a neighborhood center, where the teachers are all older Maoris, usually grandparents.

a. reason

b. example

_____ adults can learn is by attending week-long classes.

a. reason

b. example

Excerpt Two

Main Idea: There are several reasons why _____.

_____ sometimes the government makes it illegal to teach the language in school.

a. reason

b. example

_____ before 1987, it was illegal to teach the Hawaiian language in Hawaii's public schools.

a. reason

b. example

■ GO TO MyEnglishLab FOR MORE SKILL PRACTICE.

STEP 1: Organize

Work in pairs. List the examples from Listening Two for each idea from Listening One.

WHY ARE WE LOSING SO MANY LANGUAGES?	EXAMPLES FROM LISTENING TWO
1. Children don't learn the language in school.	1.
2. Children stop learning the language and only old people speak it.	2.
3. Children don't learn the culture.	3.

HOW CAN WE SAVE LANGUAGE AND CULTURES?	EXAMPLES FROM LISTENING TWO
1. Children learn the language and culture.	1.
2. The government makes the language official.	2.
3. Adults learn the language and culture.	3.

STEP 2: Synthesize

Work with the same partner. Student A, you are a student asking questions; Student B, you are the professor giving examples. Begin by asking about the reasons for language loss and then ask about ways to save languages and cultures. If the answer is not complete, ask a follow-up question such as "Could you give me an example?" Then switch roles. Use the information from Step 1.

Example

A: Why are we losing so many languages?

B: One reason for language loss is because children don't learn their native language in school.

A: Could you give me an example?

B: Before, Maori children only learned English in school, so they couldn't speak Maori with their grandparents. Now, they learn Maori and English.

A: How can we save language and culture?

B: Children can go to language programs.

A: What's an example of a language program?

B: One example is language nests.

GO TO MyEnglishLab TO CHECK WHAT YOU LEARNED.

3 FOCUS ON SPEAKING

VOCABULARY

REVIEW

Complete the conversation between two students with words from the box. Use the underlined words to help you. Then practice reading the conversation aloud with a partner. Switch roles after item 5.

acquire	extinct	official languages
disappear	~~linguists~~	preserve
dominant	native language	replacing
endangered		

A: Have you heard of the Endangered Language Alliance?

B: No, what is it?

A: It's a project of <u>people who study languages</u>. It's a group of _____linguists_____?

B: What do they do?

A: They are studying _____ languages that may die soon. And they do it
                                     1.
    in New York.

B: New York! Really? Why New York?

A: Well, English is <u>the main language</u>.

B: Right. English is the _____ language.
                                  2.

A: Yes. But some linguists believe there are as many as 800 languages spoken in New York.

B: Eight hundred languages. Wow!

A: They call New York an "endangerment hot spot." New York is full of languages that are

    <u>not going to be around in 20 or 30 years</u>.

B: Languages that will be _____?
                                   3.

(continued on next page)

A: Right. Over time, people will stop speaking the languages. The languages will slowly

go away.

B: And they will _____.
4.

A: That's right. The United Nations keeps a list of languages that might become extinct.

UN experts and linguists think that a language will probably disappear in one

generation or two. That happens when the number of people who use the language

as a first language is too small.

B: In other words, when there are not enough people who use the language as a

_____.
5.

A: Right, and when no one is learning the language, children don't

_____ it. For example, one language spoken in New York,
6.

Garifuna, is from Belize and Honduras in Central America. But people now speak

Spanish and English instead, which are the dominant languages.

B: Spanish and English are _____ Garifuna?
7.

A: Yes. And in many Central American countries, Spanish and English are the languages

the government uses.

B: So English and Spanish are the _____.
8.

A: Right. But Garifuna is now as common in New York as in Honduras and Belize where

it is from. Many people moved to New York and still speak the language. People in

New York now have classes in Garifuna.

B: Maybe they can _____ it, and they can do it in New York.
9.

They don't have to travel to far away countries.

A: Exactly!

1 Read the article from a language preservation website.

PRESERVING THE WORLD'S LANGUAGES

ENDANGERED LANGUAGES

LEARN MORE

MAKE A CONTRIBUTION

SEARCH

CONTACT US

EMAIL PAGE

PRINT PAGE

1 In 1999, the United Nations made February 21 International Mother Language Day to celebrate the many languages of the world and to encourage their preservation.

2 But preserving the world's languages is a big challenge. Languages are becoming extinct very quickly because people are starting to speak other languages, such as English. English is the dominant language of international business. Also, English and a few other languages are beginning to (1) **take over** popular entertainment, such as television, music, film, and the Internet. For example, more than 50 percent of websites on the Internet are in English. In many countries, students no longer learn in their (2) **mother tongue** at school. In addition, many parents encourage their children to learn the language of a more powerful community in order to get an education and find a good job. For these reasons, many people don't become (3) **fluent** in their native language or (4) **pass it down** to their children. This is why linguists are (5) **making an effort** to preserve the world's languages before they are lost.

www.preservethelanguages.org

2 Write the number of each boldfaced word or phrase in the text next to its definition.

_____ **a.** native language

_____ **b.** give something to younger people

_____ **c.** trying to do something

_____ **d.** gain control of

_____ **e.** speaking or writing in an easy, smooth way

Work with a partner. Choose one of the situations below. Role-play the situation using the words in the box. Then switch roles. Practice both role plays, and then perform your best role play for the class.

bilingual	make an effort	pass down
endangered	mother tongue	preserve
extinct	native language	take over
fluent		

Situation 1

Student A, you are a parent. Your native language is endangered. You want your child to learn your native language at school, but the school only teaches English. You want the school to teach your native language.

Student B, you are the school's principal. You think all of the children should learn English at school because it is the dominant language in your community.

Situation 2

Student A, you are a parent. Your native language is endangered. You want your child to go to a community program to learn your native language, but your child does not want to go.

Student B, you are the child. You only want to learn English because all the children at your school speak it. You do not want to go to a community program.

◼▪◼▪◼▪◼▪◼▪◼▪◼▪◼▪◼▪◼▪◼▪◼▪◼▪◼▪◼▪◼▪◼ GO TO MyEnglishLab FOR MORE VOCABULARY PRACTICE.

GRAMMAR

1 Read the conversation and underline the verbs. Then answer the questions.

A: What is going to happen to the language?

B: The language is probably going to disappear.

A: Will children stop learning the language?

B: Yes, they probably will.

1. What is the tense in each question? How do you know?

2. Look at each verb after *will* and *be going to* in the conversation. What is its form?

FUTURE WITH *WILL* AND *BE GOING TO*

1. Use *will* or *be going to* to . . .	What **will happen** to endangered languages?
• state facts about the future.	Some languages **will die**. Others **are going to replace** them.
• make predictions about the future.	
2. Use *be going to* to . . .	**Are** you **going to study** another language?
• talk about future plans	Yes, I**'m going to take** an English class next year.
3. To form statements with *will* or *be going to* . . .	Maori children **will be** bilingual. They **are going to speak** two languages.
• use *will* or *be going to* plus the base form of the verb.	**They'll** speak both Maori and English.

• use the **contraction** of *will* (*'ll*) with pronouns in speaking.	**She'll** be able to speak with her grandparents.
	    A: Will they save their culture?
	    B: Yes, they **will**.

• do not use contractions in affirmative short answers.	**They're going to** speak both Maori and English.
• use the **contraction** of *be going to* in speaking and informal writing.	**She's going to** be able to speak with her grandparents.
4. To form a negative statement with *will* . . .	In Greenland, students **will not lose** their native language.
• use *will not* or *won't* plus the base form of the verb.	They **won't lose** their native language.
• use *won't* in negative short answers.	**A:** Will they lose their language? **B:** No, they **won't**.
5. To form a negative statement with *be going to* . . .	In Greenland, students **are not going to lose** their native language.
• use *be not going to* or the contraction plus the base form of the verb.	They **aren't going to lose** their native language.
• use contractions in negative short answers.	**A:** Are they going to lose their language? **B:** No, they **aren't**.
6. Use *will* or *be going to* to ask questions about the future.	
• *Yes / no* questions: use *will* + subject + base form of the verb	**Will** they learn a new language?
• *Yes / no* questions: use *be* + subject + *going to* + base form of the verb	**Are we going to lose** the language?
• *Wh-* questions: begin the question with a *wh-* word	*Where* **will we study?** **When are we going to learn** the language?

(continued on next page)

7. Use *probably* to . . .

- say that you think something will happen, but you are not sure.

Fifty percent or more of languages **are probably going to be** extinct in 100 years.

Many languages **probably aren't going to survive**.

When a language dies, the culture **will probably die**, too.

When a language dies, the culture **probably won't survive**.

2 Work in groups of three. Read the questions. Each of you will make predictions using *will*, *be going to*, and *probably*. Write the other students' answers and reasons for their predictions.

QUESTIONS	NAME	NAME
1. Is your native language going to disappear, or is it going to be preserved for future generations?		
2. Will the children in your family be bilingual?		
3. Are the children in your family going to speak the same language as your grandparents?		
4. Will you stop speaking your native language?		
5. Is language going to change because of the Internet?		
6. Will new languages appear?		

GO TO MyEnglishLab FOR MORE GRAMMAR PRACTICE.

PRONUNCIATION

USING CONTRACTIONS AND REDUCTIONS WITH *WILL* AND *BE GOING TO*

When you speak, you can use the contraction *'ll* for *will*, **won't** for *will not* and the reduction *"gonna"* for *going to*.

🎧 Listen to the examples and repeat.

When my children start school, **they'll** learn Maori.
My children **won't** forget Maori, because **I'll** speak it at home.
I'm going to teach my children my native language. **It's going to be** fun!
We**'re not going to** stop speaking our native language.
Our language **isn't going to** disappear.

WILL:
Use contractions with pronouns and *will*: *I'll, you'll, he'll, she'll, it'll, we'll, they'll*

When the word before *will* ends in a consonant, pronounce it /l/ and join it to the preceding word. The underlined words in the sentence below sound the same.

🎧 Listen to the example and repeat.

<u>Nick'll</u> give me a <u>nickel</u>.

The contraction *'ll* is usually written only after pronouns. Even when the full form *will* is written, it is usually pronounced as a contraction.

We Write: What will you do?
We Say: "Whattul" you do?

BE GOING TO:
Use contractions with pronouns and *be*: *I'm, you're, it's, he's, she's, they're, we're*

We Write: What are you going to do?
We Say: "What're" you "gonna" do?

Use *"gonna"* for *going to* + base form of a verb.

---

1 🎧 **Listen and repeat the sentences. Use the contraction 'll for *will* and "gonna" for *be going to*.**

1. When I have children, I'll make sure they speak Maori. We're going to speak the same language.

2. When she goes to school, she's going to study only English.

3. If you go to Greenland, you'll hear two languages.

4. If the language dies, the culture won't survive.

5. He'll visit his native country.

6. How will you learn the language?

7. Are you going to go to a language school?

8. Will you become fluent?

2 Work with a partner. Student A, ask one of the questions. Student B, listen to the question, choose the correct answer, and read it aloud. Use the contractions **'ll** for *will* or **"gonna"** for *be going to*. Switch roles after item 4.

Student A

1. How will children learn Maori in New Zealand?

2. How will adults learn Maori?

3. What will children learn in language nests?

4. Who will teach the adults?

5. Are Maori children going to be able to speak to their grandparents in Maori?

6. Why won't children speak English to their grandparents?

7. What will happen to Maori culture if the Maori language dies?

8. Where are children going to speak the Maori language?

Student B

a. Yes, they're going to be able to speak to their grandparents.

b. They'll learn Maori language and culture.

c. They'll go to language nests and learn it in school.

d. Because they won't understand the children.

e. The culture will disappear.

f. They'll go to language classes.

g. Older Maoris will teach classes for adults.

h. They're going to speak at home and at school.

SPEAKING SKILL

GIVING REASONS AND EXAMPLES

Reasons and examples are used to explain general statements.

General Statement: Sometimes governments make it illegal to teach a native language in school.

Reason: This is because the government wants children to learn a different language.

Example: For example, before 1987 it was illegal to teach the Hawaiian language in Hawaii's public schools. This is because the government wanted children to learn in English.

Here, the speaker first makes a statement: He says that the teaching of language can be illegal. He gives an example of the Hawaiian language. Then he explains the reason.

Giving Reasons	Giving Examples
This is because . . .	For instance, . . .
The reason(s) for this is / are . . .	For example, . . .
One reason is . . .	An example of this is . . .

Work with a partner. Student A, look at this page. Student B, go to page 191 and follow the instructions there. Student A, ask the questions below. Student B will answer based on the information given on page 191. Ask follow-up questions with **why** to find out the reasons.

Example

A: Why do languages become endangered?

B: Well, sometimes governments make it illegal to teach a language in school.

A: Why is that?

B: This is because the government wants children to learn the dominant language. For example, before 1987 it was illegal to teach the Hawaiian language in Hawaii's public schools. The government wanted children to learn in English.

Student A's Questions

1. What are people doing to save endangered languages?

2. What is happening to Native American languages?

Now switch roles. Student B asks you questions. Answer each question based on the information below. Make sure you use the phrases for giving reasons and examples.

Student A's Information

3. India doesn't have a single official language.

   The government wants the different states to choose their own official languages.

   Telugu and Urdu are the official languages in the state of Andhra Pradesh.

4. Many native languages in Australia are nearly extinct.

   Only a few adults speak them.

   Only about 12 adults are fluent speakers of Wambaya, and no children are learning it.

■■■■■■■■■■■■■■■■ *GO TO* MyEnglishLab *FOR MORE SKILL PRACTICE AND TO CHECK WHAT YOU LEARNED.*

FINAL SPEAKING TASK

In this activity, you will have a small group discussion. You will discuss the future of some endangered languages and ways to preserve them. Try to use the vocabulary, grammar, pronunciation, and language for giving reasons and examples that you learned in the unit.*

Work in a small group. Follow the steps.

STEP 1: Look at the information about the endangered languages in the chart. Discuss the languages and why they are endangered.

- Predict the future of the language. Use *will, be going to* and *probably*. Give reasons and examples to support your ideas. Suggest things that you will do to save the language.

Example

ENDANGERED LANGUAGE:	**Mohawk**
NUMBER OF SPEAKERS:	About 3,000 fluent speakers
LOCATION:	North America: Ontario (Canada) and New York (United States)
DOMINANT LANGUAGE:	English
LANGUAGE PROGRAMS:	Some language programs in local schools and after school. There are classes for adults to learn the language. There are resources online, like a weekly blog of Mohawk vocabulary. There is an app to help people learn Mohawk vocabulary and pronunciation.

A: Why is Mohawk endangered?

B: It's endangered because only about 3,000 people speak Mohawk. Most Mohawk people speak English.

C: Do you think it will disappear soon?

B: I think it might because there aren't enough young people learning the language.

A: What will you do to preserve it?

B: There are some programs for adults to learn Mohawk, and other technology, like apps. I'll develop more apps.

C: I'll start language nests for young children.

---

*For Alternative Speaking Topics, see page 191.

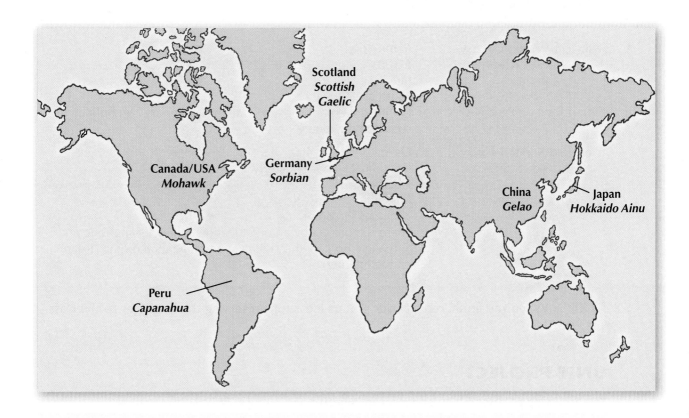

ENDANGERED LANGUAGES AND PROGRAMS TO PRESERVE THEM

a. ENDANGERED LANGUAGE: ***Sorbian***
NUMBER OF SPEAKERS: About 30,000, mostly adults
LOCATION: Germany
DOMINANT LANGUAGE: German
LANGUAGE PROGRAMS: Mostly used in the home
There is no government support

b. ENDANGERED LANGUAGE: ***Hokkaido Ainu***
NUMBER OF SPEAKERS: no native speakers
LOCATION: Japan
DOMINANT LANGUAGE: Japanese
LANGUAGE PROGRAMS: Not taught in schools
Some community programs

c. ENDANGERED LANGUAGE: ***Gelao***
NUMBER OF SPEAKERS: About 2,000, mostly older adults
LOCATION: southern China
DOMINANT LANGUAGE: Cantonese
LANGUAGE PROGRAMS: No language programs
Used in traditional religion

(continued on next page)

d. ENDANGERED LANGUAGE: ***Remo***
   NUMBER OF SPEAKERS: 6,500
   LOCATION: India
   DOMINANT LANGUAGE: Hindi and Oriya
   LANGUAGE PROGRAMS: Online grammar program. "Talking dictionary," an online recorded dictionary

e. ENDANGERED LANGUAGE: ***Ös***
   NUMBER OF SPEAKERS: less than 25, mostly elderly
   LOCATION: Siberia
   DOMINANT LANGUAGE: Russian
   LANGUAGE PROGRAMS: No language programs
   There is a project by an organization called "Living Tongues" to make a book of the language and digital recordings to put on the Internet

STEP 2: When you finish, report your group's ideas for preserving the languages to the class.

UNIT PROJECT

You are going to research an endangered language and culture. Follow these steps:

STEP 1: Go to the library or use the Internet. Find out about an endangered culture and language (such as the ones listed below).

Alagwa	Chamorro	Navajo	Sare	Trumai
Breton	Cornish	Rangi	Sonsorolese	Ugong

Use these questions to help you research. Take notes.

   a. What is the name of the endangered language?

   b. Where is the language spoken?

   c. How many people speak the language? How old are they?

   d. Is anything being done to preserve the language?

   e. Will this language survive?

STEP 2: Report to the class. Tell them about this language and its future.

Listening Task

Listen to your classmates' reports. Take notes and answer questions a-e above. Which languages are the most endangered? Which do you think has the greatest chance of surviving?

ALTERNATIVE SPEAKING TOPICS

Work in a small group. Discuss the questions.

1. Do you think people should do more to preserve endangered languages? Why or why not?

2. What do you think about learning English? How will it help you in the future?

3. Do you think learning English will threaten (hurt) your native language?

■■■■■■■■■■■■■■■■■■■■■■ GO TO MyEnglishLab TO DISCUSS ONE OF THE ALTERNATIVE TOPICS, WATCH A VIDEO ABOUT ENDANGERED CULTURES, AND TAKE THE UNIT 8 ACHIEVEMENT TEST. ■■■■■■■■■

SPEAKING SKILL

Student B's Information

Student B, listen to Student A's questions. Answer each question based on the information below. Make sure you use the phrases for giving reasons and examples.

1. Linguists and other interested people have started organizations to help preserve native languages.

   They are concerned that many of the world's languages may disappear.

   The Foundation for Endangered Languages helps to study and preserve native languages.

2. Many Native American languages are endangered.

   More Native Americans are speaking only English.

   The Iroquoian languages like Onandaga and Mohawk, spoken in upstate New York and parts of Canada, have been slowly dying for more than 200 years.

Now switch roles. Student B, ask the following questions. Student A will answer you based on the information given on his or her page. Ask follow-up questions with "why" to find out the reasons.

Student B's Questions

3. Does India have a single official language?

4. What is happening to the native languages in Australia?

UNIT WORD LIST

The Unit Word List is a summary of key vocabulary from the Student Book.
Words followed by an asterisk* are on the Academic Word List (AWL).

UNIT 1

career
concentrate*
creative*
factory
flavor
generation*
income*
insurance policy*

professional*
quit
relaxing*
stressful*
taste
tongue
tiring

UNIT 2

achieve*
avoid
distractions
factors*
focus*
goals*
manage
negative*
positive attitude*

pressure
procrastination
put off
research studies*
reward
strategies*
tasks*
waste

UNIT 3

be interested in
borrow
designing*
earn
equal
exchange
I bet
item*
member

necessities.
network*
provides
service
spend
stuff
That's it
used
valuable

UNIT 4

appreciate*
behavior
conducted*
confusing
courteous.
documents*
electronic *device
face-to-face
immediate
    response*

likely
manners
raised
respect (n)
rude
text*
treat

(continued on next page)

UNIT 5

absolutely
affect
be concerned
    about
be in favor of
claim
consumption*
deal with
discourage

get rid of
increase
junk food
lose weight
obesity
public health
reduce
take steps
tax

UNIT 6

brave
community*
courage
genes
ordinary
praise (v)
react*

responsible for
the right thing
risks
show concern for
turned out
unselfish
volunteer*

UNIT 7

connection
convinced
couch potato
criticize
enthusiasm
follow instructions*
illness
motivate
    (someone)

motivation*
needle
patient
physical*
put a band aid* on
simulation*
support
traditional*
treatment

UNIT 8

acquire*
bilingual
came up with
disappears
dominant*
endangered
eventually*
extinct

got together
linguists
native language
official language
policy*
preserve
replaces

GRAMMAR BOOK REFERENCES

NorthStar: Listening and Speaking Level 2, Fourth Edition	Focus on Grammar Level 2, Fourth Edition	Azar's Basic English Grammar, Fourth Edition
Unit 1 Descriptive Adjectives	**Unit 5** Descriptive adjectives	**Chapter 1** Using *Be:* 1-7 **Chapter 6** Nouns and Pronouns 6-3 **Chapter 14** Nouns and Modifiers 14-1, 14-2
Unit 2 Simple Present Tense	**Unit 8** Simple Present: Affirmative and Negative Statements **Unit 9** Simple Present: *Yes/No* Questions and Short Answers	**Chapter 3** Using the Simple Present 3-8, 3-9
Unit 3 Comparative Adjectives	**Unit 33** The Comparative	**Chapter 15** Making Comparisons
Unit 4 *Can, Could* and *Would* in Polite Requests	**Unit 31** Requests, Desires and Offers: *Would you, Could you, Can you . . . ?*	**Chapter 13** Modals, Part 2 13-5
Unit 5 Modals of Possibility (*may, might, could*)	**Unit 26** *May* or *Might* for Possibility	**Chapter 11** Expressing Future Time, Part 2 11-1
Unit 6 Simple Past Tense	**Unit 18** Simple Past: Affirmative and Negative Statements with Regular Verbs **Unit 19** Simple Past: Affirmative and Negative Statements with Irregular Verbs **Unit 20** Simple Past: *Yes/No* and *Wh-* Questions	**Chapter 8** Expressing Past Time, Part 1 8-8 **Chapter 9** Expressing Past Time, Part 2 9-1, 9-2, 9-3

(continued on next page)

NorthStar: Listening and Speaking Level 2, Fourth Edition	Focus on Grammar Level 2, Fourth Edition	Azar's Basic English Grammar, Fourth Edition
Unit 7 Modals of Advice and Necessity (*Should/ ought to/have to*)	**Unit 30** Advice: *Should, Ought to, Had better* **Unit 32** Necessity: *Have to, Don't have to, Must, Mustn't*	**Chapter 13** Modals, Part 2 13-5
Unit 8 Future with *Will* and *Be going to*	**Unit 24** *Be going to* for the future **Unit 25** *Will* for the future: Future Time Markers	**Chapter 10** Expressing Future Time, Part 1 10-1, 10-6 **Chapter 11** Expressing Future Time, Part 2 11-1

AUDIOSCRIPT

UNIT I: Offbeat Jobs

Listening One, page 5, Preview

HOST: Good afternoon everybody, and welcome to *What's My Job?*—the game show about offbeat jobs. I'm your host, Wayne Williams. Today's first contestant is Rita, an office manager from Chicago, Illinois.

RITA: Hi, Wayne. I'm so happy to be here! Hi, Mom. Hi, Dad. Hi, Joe . . .

HOST: OK, Rita. Let's get started. You're going to meet some people who will describe their jobs. Then you can ask three questions to guess each person's job. You can win $1,000 for each job you guess correctly. Are you ready? Let's welcome our first guest, Peter. OK, Peter, can you tell us a little about your job?

Page 6, Main Ideas

HOST: Good afternoon everybody, and welcome to *What's My Job?*—the game show about offbeat jobs. I'm your host, Wayne Williams. Today's first contestant is Rita, an office manager from Chicago, Illinois. (applause)

RITA: Hi, Wayne. I'm so happy to be here! Hi, Mom. Hi, Dad. Hi, Joe . . .

HOST: OK, Rita. Let's get started. You're going to meet some people who will describe their jobs. Then you can ask three questions to guess each person's job. You can win $1,000 for each job you guess correctly. Are you ready? Let's welcome our first guest, Peter. OK, Peter, can you tell us a little about your job?

PETER: Sure, Wayne. At my job, I work with food. My work is very interesting because I can enjoy good food and I can be creative.

HOST: That does sound interesting. OK Rita, go ahead and ask your three questions.

RITA: Do you work in a restaurant?

PETER: No, I don't.

RITA: Hmm . . . do you work in a bakery?

PETER: No, I don't. I work in a factory.

RITA: A factory?

HOST: OK Rita. Really concentrate now. It's your last question.

RITA: Hmm . . . Do you make food?

PETER: Yes, I help to make food.

HOST: OK. That's three questions. Now Rita, can you guess Peter's job?

RITA: Hmm . . . are you a chef?

PETER: No, I'm not a chef.

HOST: Ah, sorry Rita. So tell us, Peter. What do you do?

PETER: I'm a professional ice-cream taster.

RITA: A professional ice-cream taster?

PETER: That's right. I work in an ice-cream factory. I make sure the ice cream tastes good. I also think of interesting new flavors to make.

HOST: Gee, sounds like a difficult job, Peter. You taste ice cream all day and you get paid for it!

PETER: Yes, that's right. I'm lucky to have such a great job.

HOST: Good for you. So tell us Peter, is there anything difficult about your job?

PETER: Well . . . I guess so . . . For one thing, I can't eat all the ice cream. Otherwise, I'd get too full. I only taste a bit of ice cream and then I have to spit it out.

HOST: I see. Is there anything else that's difficult?

PETER: Let me think. Well, I have to be very careful to take care of my taste buds. For example, I can't eat spicy or hot foods.

HOST: Really?

PETER: Yes, and I don't drink alcohol or coffee . . . And I don't smoke, either. If I did those things, I might hurt my taste buds, and then I wouldn't be able to taste the ice cream very well.

HOST: Wow! You do have to be careful.

PETER: Yes, I do. In fact, my taste buds are so important that they are covered by a one million-dollar insurance policy.

HOST: One million dollars! You don't say!

PETER: That's right. You see, if I can't taste the ice cream, my company and I will lose a lot of money. That would really hurt my income.

HOST: Gee, you do have a very important job, Peter. So how did you get started as an ice-cream taster? Did you go to ice-cream tasting school?

PETER: Oh, no. My family has been in the ice-cream business for a long time. I've always wanted to work with ice cream, too.

HOST: That's great, Peter. Thank you very much for being on the show, and keep up the good work! OK everybody, it's time for a commercial break. But, don't go away!

Listening Two, Page 10, Comprehension

JOB COUNSELOR: Hello, I'm Nancy and I'll be your job counselor. I'm glad you've decided to come to this group; it's a good place to come to get ideas about new jobs or careers you might be interested in. It's helpful to listen to other people talk about their jobs when you're thinking of changing careers yourself. So, to begin, I'd like everyone to introduce themselves and tell us what your current job is and maybe why you are thinking of changing careers. I'll take some notes about what you say, which will help me suggest some possible new jobs. Hopefully, we can find the right job for you! OK. Let's start with you.

MAN: Hi, sure. My name is Mike and I'm a window washer.

JOB COUNSELOR: OK. Great. Why don't you tell me a little about your job?

MAN: Well, I wash office building windows, so I go high up in the air in a basket to reach the windows.

JOB COUNSELOR: Sounds scary to me! Do you like it? And if so, why?

MAN: Yeah, I really like my job because I enjoy being outdoors. I like to breathe the fresh air and look at the beautiful views of the city. It's really relaxing. I really don't think I could work indoors in an office or a store. And I earn a high salary . . . I make a lot of money. Window washing is a good job for me because I'm good with my hands. I don't like sitting in front of a computer all day. It was difficult for me to get started as a window washer. But I started my own business and I like that—working for myself—no boss, you know?

JOB COUNSELOR: OK . . . I'm just making some notes; like being outdoors, good with your hands, like being your own boss. OK. So why do you want a new job?

MAN: Well, my job is pretty dangerous. I have to be very careful not to fall out of the basket, and I have to be careful not to drop things on people below. I just think I'd like something a little safer. Also, I enjoy it, you know, but it's a lot of work and can be very tiring. I go home at night and just want to sleep!

JOB COUNSELOR: Hmm . . . dangerous, wants something a little safer. OK. Great. Let's hear from the next person. Please introduce yourself and tell us a little bit about your job.

WOMAN: Hi, I'm Sarah and I'm a professional shopper. I go shopping for people who are busy and don't have time to shop. Basically, people give me a shopping list and some money, and I do the shopping for them.

JOB COUNSELOR: Well, if you like to shop, sounds like a great job.

WOMAN: It has its good and bad parts. What's good about it is that I do love to shop and I really like to work with people. I'm also very good with money. I always find clothes that are on sale—you know—cheap. But, well, the bad part is that my job isn't that easy. I'm on my feet a lot, so my work is tiring. And it wasn't easy

to get started as a shopper. I worked for many years as a salesclerk in a department store. Then I started to meet people who needed a shopper. So, when I had enough customers, I quit my job at the department store and started my own business. Now, I like being my own boss. However, I have to do everything myself and it's a lot of work and it can be very stressful, you know, making all the decisions myself. So, I wish I could just go to work, do my job, and then go home at night.

JOB COUNSELOR: Yeah, sometimes it's easier to work for someone else and let them have all the headaches! OK. Let's see . . . who's next? What's your name?

Page 11, Listening Skill 1

MAN: It was difficult for me to get started as a window washer. But I started my own business and I like that—working for myself—no boss, you know?

Page 11, Listening Skill 2

Excerpt One

WOMAN: It has its good and bad parts. What's good about it is that I do love to shop and I really like to work with people. I'm also very good with money. I always find clothes that are on sale—you know—cheap. But, well, the bad part is that my job isn't that easy. I'm on my feet a lot, so my work is tiring.

Excerpt Two

WOMAN: I quit my job at the department store and started my own business. Now, I like being my own boss. However, I have to do everything myself and it's a lot of work.

Page 12, Connect the Listenings, Step One: Organize

Excerpt One

MAN: Well, I wash office building windows, so I go high up in the air in a basket to reach the windows.

JOB COUNSELOR: Sounds scary to me! Do you like it? And if so, why?

MAN: Yeah, I really like my job because I enjoy being outdoors. I like to breathe the fresh air and look at the beautiful views of the city. It's really relaxing. I really don't think I could work indoors in an office or a store. And I earn a high salary . . . I make a lot of money. Window washing is a good job for me because I'm good with my hands. I don't like sitting in front of a computer all day. It was difficult for me to get started as a window washer. But I started my own business and I like that—working for myself—no boss, you know?

JOB COUNSELOR: OK . . . I'm just making some notes; like being outdoors, good with your hands, like being your own boss. OK. So why do you want a new job?

MAN: Well, my job is pretty dangerous. I have to be very careful not to fall out of the basket, and I have to be careful not to drop things on people below. I just think I'd like something a little safer. Also, I enjoy it, you know, but it's a lot of work and can be very tiring. I go home at night and just want to sleep!

Excerpt Two

WOMAN: Hi, I'm Sarah and I'm a professional shopper. I go shopping for people who are busy and don't have time to shop. Basically, people give me a shopping list and some money, and I do the shopping for them.

JOB COUNSELOR: Well, if you like to shop, sounds like a great job.

WOMAN: It has its good and bad parts. What's good about it is that I do love to shop and I really like to work with people. I'm also very good with money. I always find clothes that are on sale—you know—cheap. But, well, the bad part is that my job isn't that easy. I'm on my feet a lot, so my work is tiring. And it wasn't easy to get started as a shopper. I worked for many years as a salesclerk in a department store. Then I started to meet people who needed a shopper. So, when I had enough customers, I quit my job at the department store and started my own business. Now, I like being my own boss. However, I have to do everything myself, and it's a lot of work and it can be very stressful, you know, making all the decisions myself. So, I wish I could just go to work, do my job, and then go home at night.

Excerpt Three

PETER: That's right. I work in an ice-cream factory. I make sure the ice cream tastes good. I also think of interesting new flavors to make.

HOST: Gee, sounds like a difficult job, Peter. You taste ice cream all day and you get paid for it!

PETER: Yes, that's right. I'm lucky to have such a great job.

HOST: Good for you. So tell us Peter, is there anything difficult about your job?

PETER: Well . . . I guess so . . . For one thing, I can't eat all the ice cream. Otherwise, I'd get too full. I only taste a bit of ice cream and then I have to spit it out.

HOST: I see. Is there anything else that's difficult?

PETER: Let me think. Well, I have to be very careful to take care of my taste buds. For example, I can't eat spicy or hot foods.

HOST: Really?

PETER: Yes, and I don't drink alcohol or coffee . . . And I don't smoke, either. If I did those things, I might hurt my taste buds, and then I wouldn't be able to taste the ice cream very well.

HOST: Wow! You do have to be careful.

PETER: Yes, I do. In fact, my taste buds are so important that they are covered by a one million-dollar insurance policy.

HOST: One million dollars! You don't say!

PETER: That's right. You see, if I can't taste the ice cream, my company and I will lose a lot of money.

UNIT 2: Where Does the Time Go?

Listening One, Page 27, Preview

COLLEGE COUNSELOR: Good morning everybody. It's great to see you here today. You know, one of the most important factors in school success is having good study habits. So, I'd like to start out by asking you all a few questions about *your* study habits. Then, later, I'll suggest some strategies that will help you study and manage your time better.

Page 28, Main Ideas I

COLLEGE COUNSELOR: Good morning everybody. It's great to see you here today. You know, one of the most important factors in school success is having good study habits. So, I'd like to start out by asking you all a few questions about *your* study habits. Then, later, I'll suggest some strategies that will help you study and manage your time better. So, how many of you like to multitask—you know, like surf the web, or chat with your friends while you study? OK . . . I see a lot of you . . . well, I hate to say this, but research studies show that multitasking has negative effects on your school success. So, the first goal you should set for yourselves is to avoid multitasking while you study. Think you can do it?

OK, so now, let's talk about another bad study habit: procrastination. Imagine this situation: You get an assignment to write a research paper for your English class, and you have two weeks to finish it. How many of you think you'll start working on it the first day? OK. . . . I see a couple of hands. How many of you will probably put it off for a few days? . . . Be honest. . . . all right, who would put it off to the last day and then stay up all night trying to finish it? . . . ahhh . . . OK. . . . Well, don't feel too bad. Researchers say that 80–95% of students procrastinate sometimes, and about 20% do it often. They also say that procrastination is getting worse. People are becoming more distracted and putting off their work more than they did in the past.

So let's talk about some strategies to help you avoid those problems and manage your time better.

OK, so the first thing you need to do is to set goals. That means, you need to think about all of the tasks you need or want to get done. Write them all down.

The next step is to put your list of goals in order from most important to least important. So, for example, your math homework needs to come before seeing that new movie, right?

The third step is to use a calendar to plan your time. Schedule all of your tasks, and be sure to give yourself plenty of time to do them. And be careful with big assignments—like that English paper—you can't do it all at once, right? No, you need to divide it into smaller tasks that you can do one at a time. Also, don't forget to schedule things like exercising, getting enough sleep, seeing friends. Those are important too! OK, so tell me, does anybody have any questions so far? No?

OK, so, finally comes the hard part—avoiding distractions and getting your work done. But how can you do it? Well, there's no one right answer. You need to find what works for you. But, here are a few strategies you can try:

One idea is the "Do Nothing" strategy. This strategy has two rules. The first rule is "you don't have to do your work." That's right. . . . but there's another rule. The second rule is "you can't do anything else." So, when your two choices are your work or nothing, it's easy, but the problem is it's so easy to get distracted . . . phones, friends, the Internet . . . right?

So another strategy is to remove all of your distractions: turn off your phone—hide it in another room if you have to. Put away the video games. Turn off your Internet. Do whatever you need to avoid distractions.

A third strategy is to promise yourself a reward when you finish your work. For example, tell yourself you can go to the party on Saturday after you get your homework done.

A final suggestion comes from Piers Steele, who is a researcher and a procrastinator himself—in fact, he took 10 years to finish his study on procrastination!— He suggests this: Give some money to another person and tell the person that if you don't finish your work on time, they can give the money away. They can give it to a stranger, or even worse, to someone you *don't* like. Now that should keep you working!

Page 31, Make Inferences

Excerpt One

CC: Imagine this situation: You get an assignment to write a research paper for your English class, and you have two weeks to finish it. How many of you think you'll start working on it the first day? OK. . . . I see a couple of hands.

Excerpt Two

CC: Also, don't forget to schedule things like exercising, getting enough sleep, seeing friends. Those are important too! OK, so tell me, does anybody have any questions so far? No?

Excerpt Three

CC: OK, so, finally comes the hard part—avoiding distractions and getting your work done. But how can you do it? Well, there's no one right answer. You need to find what works for you.

Listening Two, page 34, Comprehension

COUNSELOR: OK, so now, I'd like you to work together in groups to discuss your own study habits. Group leaders, I'll ask you to report back about your group's answers in a few minutes. Any questions? . . . OK, go ahead and get started.

STUDENT 1: Hi, I guess I'm our leader. My name's Annie.

STUDENT 2: Hi, I'm Sam.

STUDENT 3: I'm Justin.

STUDENT 1: Hey . . . so why'd you guys decide to take this workshop?

STUDENT 2: Well, me, I'm here because . . . well, I'm not doing so well in school right now, and I need to improve my grades. My counselor said this workshop would help, but I don't know. I think we're wasting our time.

STUDENT 1: Really? You think so? I hope it's gonna be useful. I wanna go to medical school, so it's really important for me to do well in school. So, Justin, how about you?

STUDENT 3: Me? Well I'm here because my parents told me to sign up. They said I have to get straight A's, or else . . .

STUDENT 2: Whoa, are you kidding? That's some serious pressure.

STUDENT 3: Yeah, tell me about it.

STUDENT 1: OK, we'd better get started . . . so, our first question is:" Do you multitask while you study or attend class?

STUDENT 2: Well, yeah, I do, for sure. I text my friends during class a lot . . . especially during long boring lectures. It's hard to concentrate.

STUDENT 1: Yeah, it is easy to get distracted, especially if you have your phone or computer right there. Sometimes I surf the web when I'm working on the computer. How about you, Justin?

STUDENT 3: Me too. I also like to listen to music, and I chat online while I do my homework. And sometimes I take breaks to play video games.

STUDENT 1: Sounds like multi-tasking to me!

STUDENT 3: Well, doesn't everybody? I don't really think it's all that bad for you. I mean, we made it to college right?

STUDENT 1: Well, yeah, I guess so . . . OK, so . . . our next question is "Do you procrastinate?

STUDENT 2: Well, yeah, I put off hard assignments. Sometimes I just don't know how to get started. And besides, there're so many fun things to do in college!

STUDENT 1: That's true, but for me, I hate putting things off. It's too stressful. Besides, I think you need to think about what you want to achieve after college. I try to think about my goal to become a doctor and that helps me focus on my schoolwork.

STUDENT 3: Wow. You have a positive attitude. I put off work that I don't like to do, like writing papers. And, yeah, I guess I do waste time playing video games when I don't feel like studying.

STUDENT 1: Yeah . . . OK, so our last question: "Which strategies do you want to try?" Me, I'm definitely gonna set goals and schedule my time better.

STUDENT 2: Really? All that stuff about lists and schedules sounds like too much work! I do think I'll start putting my phone away during class though.

STUDENT 3: I need to stop procrastinating. But, I'll tell you I'm NOT gonna start giving my money away! Maybe I'll start giving myself a reward for getting stuff done . . . like buying myself a new video game!

STUDENT 1: Ha! Sounds like a great idea!

Page 35, Listening Skill 2

Excerpt One

STUDENT 2: Well, yeah, I put off hard assignments. Sometimes I just don't know how to get started. And besides, there're so many fun things to do in college!

STUDENT 1: That's true, but for me, I hate putting things off. It's too stressful.

Excerpt Two

STUDENT 1: OK, so our last question: "Which strategies do you want to try?" Me, I'm definitely gonna set goals and schedule my time better.

STUDENT 2: Really? All that stuff about lists and schedules sounds like too much work!

UNIT 3: A Penny Saved Is a Penny Earned

Listening One, page 52, Preview

WOMAN 1: Good morning, everyone. Let's get started . . . My name is Carol, and I'd like to welcome you to the City Barter Network. I'm glad you all could come to today's meeting. And I'm really happy to see so many people who are interested in joining our network. Now, there are a few things I'd like to do this morning.

Page 53, Main Ideas, 1

WOMAN 1: First, I want to tell you a little about bartering—what bartering is. Then I'll explain how you can barter in our network. Well, then, if you want to join, I'll sign you up as a member. Any questions? OK. Let's get started. First of all, does anyone know what bartering is?

MAN 1: Bartering is trading stuff, right? Like, I trade my car for your computer, or something like that?

WOMAN 1: Well, that's one kind of bartering— exchanging one item for another item—but in our barter network, we only exchange services—things you can do for another person.

MAN 1: Oh, I see.

WOMAN 1: Well, here's how it works. First, when you join the network, you sign your name on our member list and you list all of the services you can provide. Then every member gets a copy of the list or they can read it on our website.

MAN 2: So, what kinds of services do members provide?

WOMAN 1: Well, most members provide services that a lot of people need like cooking, cleaning, or fixing things. But, ah . . . well, some people provide more unusual services like taking photographs, designing a website, or even giving music lessons.

WOMAN 2: Music lessons?! So, do you think I could get piano lessons? I've always wanted to learn how to play the piano.

WOMAN 1: Yeah, sure.

WOMAN 2: Wow! That's great!

WOMAN 1: It sure is! But remember that when you barter, you need to *provide* a service before you can *get* one . . . So that brings me to the next step, how to barter. After you become a member, another member can ask you to provide a service, to do something for them. For every hour of work you do for someone, you earn one Time Dollar.

MAN 1: So, you can earn money?

WOMAN 1: Well, no, you can't. Time Dollars aren't *real* money. Basically, each Time Dollar just equals one hour of time that you spend providing a service. Later, you can spend your Time Dollars to get a service from someone else.

MAN 1: So all the members earn one Time Dollar per hour, no matter what kind of work they do?

WOMAN 1: Yes. That's right. In our network, everyone's time is equal. No service is more valuable than another one. Oh, here, let me give you an example. A few weeks ago another member needed some help cleaning his house. I spent three hours cleaning his house, so I earned three Time Dollars. Then last week, my computer broke and I needed to get it fixed. So I called another member who fixed it for me. He spent one hour fixing it, so I spent one Time Dollar. It was great! I saved money because I didn't need to pay anyone to fix it for me.

Man 1: I have a question . . . What if you don't know how to do anything? I mean I don't really have any skills . . .

Woman 2: Hmm . . . can you walk?

Man 1: Walk? Well, of course I can walk . . .

Woman 2: OK, it's a deal. You can do dog-walking! I need someone to take my dog for a walk when I'm not home. Why don't you do it? . . .

Man 1: Well, I suppose I could . . .

Woman 1: Great! It looks like you're all ready to barter! But, let's get signed up first. Next, I'll pass out some forms . . .

Page 54, Make Inferences

Excerpt One

Man 1: Bartering is trading stuff, right? Like, I trade my car for your computer, or something like that?

Woman 1: Well, that's one kind of bartering—exchanging one item for another item—but in our barter network, we only exchange services—things you can do for another person.

Man 1: Oh, I see.

Excerpt Two

Man 1: I have a question . . . What if you don't' know how to do anything? I mean I don't really have any skills . . .

Woman 2: Hmm . . . can you walk?

Man 1: Walk? Well, of course I can walk.

Listening Two, page 57, Comprehension

Man: Hi there. I'm Mark.

Woman: Oh hi. I'm Natalie. It's nice to meet you.

Man: So, Natalie, tell me, why did you decide to join the City Barter Network?

Woman: Oh, well, I was looking for someone to fix my car. Luckily, I found somebody, and now I think I'm going to barter for piano lessons, too. How about you?

Man: Well, I'm looking for people to barter with because I belong to another group called the Compact.

Woman: The Compact? What's that?

Man: We're a group of people that made a compact—you know, like a promise . . . we promised not to buy anything new for a year.

Woman: No kidding! You aren't going to buy *anything* new for a whole year?

Man: Well . . . actually we *can* buy new necessities, things, you know, that you *need* for your health and safety . . . for example, food and medicine.

Woman: That sounds hard. So why did you decide to do it?

Man: Well, we decided that we were spending too much money on *things*, you know . . . clothes, cars, electronics . . . we think most people just have too much *stuff* . . . *stuff* that they really don't need. We wanted to stop buying so much and learn to live with less.

Woman: I see . . . But you need to buy *some* things beside food and medicine . . . How do you get the *other* stuff you need?

Man: Well, we either borrow things from other people, or we buy things used at thrift stores . . . or we barter for the stuff we need.

Woman: Huh . . . so how's it going? Are you keeping your promise?

Man: Yeah . . . mostly . . . though sometimes we just *have* to buy something new when we can't borrow it or find it used . . . like, for instance, I needed to buy some new paint for my house. But that's it so far.

Woman: Wow! I bet you're saving a lot of money! How many members are in the Compact?

Man: It started out with only ten people but now there are thousands of members all over the world. . . . You should join us. You can do it online at our website.

Woman: Well . . . thanks, but I don't think I could do it. I like shopping too much—especially for new clothes! But hey, good luck!

Page 58, Listening Skill 2

Excerpt One

Man: Well, we decided that we were spending too much money on *things*, you know . . . clothes, cars, electronics . . . we think most people just have too much *stuff* . . . stuff that they really don't need. We wanted to stop buying so much and learn to live with less.

Woman: I see . . . But you need to buy *some* things beside food and medicine . . . How do you get the *other* stuff you need?

Excerpt Two

Woman: Huh . . . so how's it going? Are you keeping your promise?

Man: Yeah . . . mostly . . . though sometimes we just *HAVE* to buy something new when we can't borrow it or find it used . . . like, for instance, I needed to buy some new paint for my house. But that's it so far.

Page 67, Pronunciation 3

1. $7.50
2. $83.25
3. $319.40
4. $16.99
5. $1,500

UNIT 4: What Happened to Etiquette?

Listening One, page 75, Preview

HOST: Today our guest is Sarah Jones, a reporter who recently did an international study of manners. Welcome.

SARAH JONES: Thank you. It's great to be here.

HOST: So, Sarah, why did you decide to study manners?

SARAH JONES: Well, I wanted to find out if what is happening to manners. I wanted to know…are people really becoming less polite? So, I decided to conduct a test to find out.

HOST: Hmmm . . . I see. It seems like it'd be hard to test manners though. How did you do it?

Page 76, Main Ideas

HOST: Today our guest is Sarah Jones, a reporter who recently did an international study of manners. Welcome.

SARAH JONES: Thank you. It's great to be here.

HOST: So, Sarah, why did you decide to study manners?

SARAH JONES: Well, I wanted to find out what is happening to manners. I wanted to know, . . . are people really becoming less polite? So, I decided to conduct a test to find out.

HOST: Hmmm . . . I see. It seems like it'd be hard to test manners though. How did you do it?

SARAH JONES: Well, another reporter and I traveled to large cities in 35 different countries around the world—and in each city we observed people's language and behavior to see how courteous they were.

HOST: Hmmm . . . OK, so how did you conduct these tests?

SARAH JONES: First, we did a "door test," and then a "document drop," and finally, a "customer service" test. We did 60 tests in all—20 of each kind. In the door test, we wanted to see whether or not people would hold the door open for us as we entered or left a building. In the document drop, one of us dropped a file folder full of documents. We wanted to see if people would help us pick them up. And for the customer service test,

we wanted to find out if people working in stores were polite—so we noticed if the cashiers were courteous and if they said "thank you,"

HOST: So, what did you find out?

SARAH JONES: Well, the results were really different depending on the city . . .

HOST: OK, so tell us about the most courteous city . . .

SARAH JONES: OK, in the most courteous city, 90 percent of the people passed the door test.

HOST: Wow! You mean to say 90 percent of the people held the door open for you?

SARAH JONES: Yeah, that's right.

HOST: Well, I guess holding the door for someone is an easy enough thing to do.

SARAH JONES: Well, true, but sometimes people aren't sure if they should hold the door open . . . I mean, how long should you hold the door for someone who is behind you but still far away?

HOST: Yeah, that's true. . . .

SARAH JONES: So, almost everyone held the *door*. But only 55 percent of the people helped us pick up our papers.

HOST: Huh, only 55 percent? That's not very good. But, I can imagine that sometimes you just can't help. I mean, what if your hands are full?

SARAH JONES: Yes, but one woman had two cups of coffee on a tray and her keys and wallet in the other hand. She put everything in one hand and helped! The reporter wanted to help her!

HOST: Huh, interesting! OK, now, what about customer service?

SARAH JONES: So, in the most polite city, we went to different locations of a popular coffee shop to test the cashiers, and it turns out that 19 out of 20 of them said "thank you."

HOST: So did they just do it because they're being paid to be polite?

SARAH JONES: Well, that's true, they are trained to be courteous. But some said they do it because it shows respect.

HOST: You know, what I'm curious about is why some people are courteous and some others aren't. Did you ask people why they were polite?

SARAH JONES: Yeah, actually, we did. *Most* people who passed the test said they were raised to be courteous; they were taught good manners when they were young. And some people said they just try to treat people the same way they want to be treated. They appreciate it when others take the time to help them when they need it, so they want to do the same. You know—they follow the "golden rule."

Host: Hmmm . . . So what did you learn about the different people in your study? Are some people more likely to help than others?

Sarah Jones: Yeah, this is where it gets interesting. We tested all kinds of people: young, old, men, women, business people, students, police officers . . . anyone and everyone! And actually, age or career didn't really matter, but we did find that men helped more often than women, especially in the document drop tests. In that test, men offered to help 63 percent of the time, compared to only 47 percent for women. Also, the men were much more likely to help me compared to the other reporter . . . who was male. So, it seems like men are more likely to help a woman than another man.

Host: Well, I suppose that's not so surprising. OK, so now, we've been waiting . . . of the 35 cities you visited, which city won—which one was the most polite?

Sarah Jones: Well . . . You're not going to believe this . . . It was New York City!

Host: You're kidding! New York certainly isn't known for good manners. I'm so surprised!

Sarah Jones: We were too, but New York won!

Page 78, Make Inferences

Excerpt One

Woman: So, *almost everyone* held the *door*. But only *55 percent* of the people helped us pick up our *papers*.

Excerpt Two

Woman: In that test, *men* offered to help *63* percent of the time, compared to only *47* percent for *women*

Listening Two, page 80, Comprehension

Host: Now is the time for listeners to call in and tell *us* what *they* think. We've just heard about an interesting study of manners. So the question for our listeners is, why do you think there's a lack of manners? Caller one, you're on.

Caller 1: Hi. Well, I learned how to behave at home . . . from my parents. I think that's where a lot of people learn manners. But nowadays, parents are too busy; some moms or dads are raising children alone or have two jobs and just aren't home much. So there's less family time and that's where you learn manners—from your family, at home.

Host: Yeah, good point. Parents don't spend enough time with their kids, teaching them good manners. Well, let's see what other callers have to say. Who's next?

Caller 2: Well, I live in a large city and one thing I notice is there are people living here from all over the world. When I walk down the street, I hear people speaking three or four different languages.

Host: So it's because we don't all speak the same language? That's why people are rude?

Caller 2: No, not that. Manners are cultural, right?

Host: Right. Sure.

Caller 2: And what's polite in one culture might not be polite in another. So when many people live together, sometimes it's hard to know what's right and wrong . . . I mean, sometimes I can't tell if someone is being rude, or if they just learned to behave differently in their own culture. It gets confusing.

Host: Yeah, that's true. It is confusing when different cultures follow different rules of etiquette . . . OK. Let's take one more call.

Caller 3: Why are people rude? Electronic devices. I think it's because of cell phones, texting, and the Internet.

Host: Well, you certainly have a strong opinion!

Caller 3: Look, everywhere you go you see people talking on cell phones or texting; they're having a conversation with someone who isn't even there!

Host: Well, maybe, but cell phones and texting are very convenient.

Caller 3: Sure, but people have forgotten how to talk with someone face to face. Also, people expect an immediate response and they don't see a need to be courteous; they just write short messages. They forget to say things like, "how are you" and "thank you."

Host: I don't know. I like getting a fast response. Sometimes it's nice to not have a long conversation.

Caller 3: Look, I have a cell phone and I use text messages and I think they are useful. But I think people use them too much. Electronic devices have made us more separate; now we spend more time on our devices and less time with real people.

Host: Well, we're out of time but to wrap up: we need more family time, a better understanding of our different cultures, and more face-to-face time . . . certainly some things to think about! That's all for now, until next week.

Page 81, Listening Skill

Excerpt One

Caller 2: And what's polite in one culture might not be polite in another. So when many people live together, sometimes it's hard to know what's right and wrong. I mean, sometimes I can't tell if someone is being rude, or if they just learned to behave differently in their own culture. It gets confusing.

Host: Yeah, that's true. It is confusing when different cultures follow different rules of etiquette.

Excerpt Two

CALLER 1: Hi. Well, I learned how to behave at home . . . from my parents. I think that's where a lot of people learn manners. But these days, parents are too busy; some moms or dads are raising children alone or have two jobs and just aren't home much. So there's less family time and that's where you learn manners—from your family, at home.

HOST: Yeah, good point. Parents don't spend enough time with their kids, teaching them good manners.

UNIT 5: The Fat Tax

Listening One, page 97, Preview

HOST: Good afternoon, and welcome to "The Nation Talks." Today's topic is in the news a lot lately—the increase in obesity in the United States. Two thirds of Americans today are overweight or obese, and most health researchers believe that almost half will be obese by 2030. Clearly, obesity is a very serious public health problem. On today's show, we'll be discussing several ways to deal with obesity.

Page 98, Main Ideas

HOST: Good afternoon, and welcome to "The Nation Talks." Today's topic is in the news a lot recently—the increase in obesity in the United States. Two thirds of Americans today are overweight or obese, and most health researchers believe that almost half will be obese by 2030. Clearly, obesity is a very serious public health problem. On today's show, we'll be discussing several ways to deal with obesity.

Let me get the conversation started by introducing our first guest, reporter Roberta Anderson. Roberta is researching one way to deal with the problem of obesity—a "fat tax." Roberta, could you please explain what a fat tax is?

ROBERTA ANDERSON (RA): Certainly. Basically, a fat tax is a special tax on foods with a lot of sugar or fat in them. This includes unhealthy foods such as butter, and junk food, such as chips, soda, and cookies.

HOST: So if I understand correctly, a fat tax makes unhealthy foods more expensive. And then fewer people buy them?

RA: Yes, exactly—the idea is to discourage people from buying food that can make them obese.

HOST: And did anyone try this before?

RA: Yes. For example, Denmark introduced a tax on foods with a lot of fat in them. The tax was not just on junk food like chips and cookies, but also on basic foods like butter, cheese, and meat. Recently another European country, Hungary, also added a tax on certain high fat foods, and increased taxes on soda and alcohol. However, you should know that the fat tax in Denmark lasted for only one year, and then, the government got rid of it.

HOST: Really? And why was that?

RA: Mostly because of the costs. Shoppers were unhappy about the higher prices. And small business owners claimed that about 1,300 people lost their jobs when customers stopped shopping in Denmark and went to Germany to buy food. Interestingly, however, maybe the tax did have an effect on the way people in Denmark eat.

HOST: Really? What kind of an effect?

RA: Well, their consumption of butter, margarine, and oil went down by 10–20% in the three months after the government added the tax.

HOST: How much? 10%?

RA: Ten to TWENty percent

HOST: Well, that's quite a bit. Do you mean that they got rid of the tax because of the costs, not public health?

RA: Well, yes—at least that's what many people believe. Several studies show that fat taxes might work. One British study, for example, shows that a 20% tax on soda could reduce obesity by 3.5%. Another study in the U.S. shows that an 18% tax on pizza and soda could help the average American lose weight, maybe even five pounds per year.

HOST: Wait a minute—Five pounds a year? Those are pretty big changes! So, you're saying that taxing unhealthy food will change people's eating habits that much?

RA: No, I'm saying that MAYBE taxes make a difference—or at least that is what some researchers claim. But remember, these are just studies. No one knows for sure what will really happen when we use these kinds of taxes.

HOST: Sorry. Let me get this straight. Didn't you just say that in Denmark the consumption of unhealthy foods went down when taxes on them went up?

RA: Yes, I DID say that, but we aren't sure that the tax was the main reason. Some researchers think that maybe the economy was the real reason people stopped buying those products.

HOST: What do you mean by "the economy"? Can you explain that?

RA: Certainly. The Danish economy was not doing well at that time—the Danish people were having money problems—so maybe people were spending less money on food in general. And when people are having money problems, they pay close attention to even small price changes.

Host: Very interesting. Well, now let's see what our listeners have to say. What's your opinion of a fat tax? Do you think it could work? Call us at 1-800. . . .

Page 100, Make Inferences

Excerpt One

Host: So, you're saying that taxing unhealthy food will change people's eating habits that much?

RA: No, I'm saying that MAYBE taxes make a difference—or at least that is what some researchers claim. But remember, these are just studies. No one knows for sure what will really happen when we use these kinds of taxes.

Excerpt Two

Host: Sorry. Let me get this straight. Didn't you just say that in Denmark the consumption of unhealthy foods went down when taxes on them went up?

RA: Yes, I did say that, but we aren't sure that the tax was the main reason.

Listening Two, page 102, Comprehension

Host: Welcome to "The Nation Talks."

Caller 1: Thank you for taking my call. First of all, let me say that I think this is a very important topic. I'm a nurse, and I work with young people. As I'm sure you know, obesity is a big problem among children in the U.S. today. One in three children is overweight or obese. I think this is a public health emergency. And in an emergency, the government needs to take steps to solve the problem.

Host: So are you saying that you are in favor of a "fat tax?"

Caller 1: Definitely. I know fat taxes may not be popular, but taxes in general work because they can really affect people's behavior—just look at the effect of cigarette taxes.

Host: Hmmm . . . Interesting comparison. Could you explain what you mean?

Caller 1: Yeah, sure. In the 1990s, the government increased taxes on cigarettes. That increased the cost of cigarettes by about 50 percent, and as a result, smoking rates went down from about 42% in the 1960s to less than 20% today.

Host: So you think that a fat tax might work as well as the taxes on cigarettes did?

Caller 1: Yes, absolutely.

Host: Ok, thanks for your call. Hello? You're on "The Nation Talks." So do you think of a "fat tax?" Do you agree with the other caller?

Caller 2: No, I'm afraid not. I just don't think that it's the government's job to tell people what they should and shouldn't eat.

Host: Well, a tax is not the same as telling people what to eat, is it?

Caller 2: In a way it is. By taxing certain types of food, the government is trying to manage people's behavior. And I don't like the government trying to control what I do. Also, it's not fair to poor people who don't have a lot of money to spend on food.

Host: But shouldn't the government be concerned about public health?

Caller 2: Yes, but I just don't think that more taxes are the answer. There are other ways.

Host: For example?

Caller 2: Well, what about parents? Shouldn't they be teaching their children about healthy eating? Why do we always look to the government to solve our problems?

Host: Very interesting. Thanks for your call . . . Let's go to Helen. Hello? Go ahead, please.

Page 103, Listening Skill

Excerpt One

RA: Well, their consumption of butter, margarine, and oil went down by 10–20% in the three months after the government added the tax.

Host: How much? 10%?

RA: Ten to TWENty percent

Excerpt Two

RA: . . . Another study in the U.S. shows that an 18% tax on pizza and soda could help the average American lose weight, maybe even five pounds per year.

Host: Wait a minute—Five pounds a year? Those are pretty big changes! So, you're saying that taxing unhealthy food will change people's eating habits that much?

RA: No, I'm saying that MAYBE taxes make a difference—or at least that is what some researchers claim.

Excerpt Three

Host: Sorry. Let me get this straight. Didn't you just say that in Denmark the consumption of unhealthy foods went down when taxes on them went up?

RA: Yes, I DID say that, but we aren't sure that the tax was the main reason.

Page 103, Connect the Listenings

Excerpt One

RA: . . . Several studies show that fat taxes might work. One British study, for example, shows that a 20% tax on soda could reduce obesity by 3.5%. Another study in the U.S. shows that an 18% tax on pizza and soda could help the average American lose weight, maybe even five pounds per year.

HOST: Wait a minute—Five pounds a year? Those are pretty big changes! So, you're saying that taxing unhealthy food will change people's eating habits that much?

Excerpt Two

CALLER 1: . . . I know fat taxes may not be popular, but taxes in general work because they can really affect people's behavior—just look at the effect of cigarette taxes.

HOST: Hmmm . . . Interesting comparison. Could you explain what you mean?

CALLER 1: Yeah, sure. In the 1990s, the government increased taxes on cigarettes. That increased the cost of cigarettes by about 50 percent, and as a result, smoking rates went down from about 42% in the 1960s to less than 20% today.

UNIT 6: Everyday Heroes

Listening One, page 121, Preview

ANNOUNCER: What does the word "hero" mean to you? Maybe you think of superheroes or famous people who do great things. But what about every day ordinary people who help others? Are they heroes too? We begin tonight's program in New York where Brad Peck has the story of the ordinary man that many people are now calling a hero.

REPORTER: It was a Tuesday afternoon at about 12:45, and subway riders were waiting on the platform for their train to arrive.

WOMAN 1: I was standing there waiting for my train, when suddenly, a young man fell down on the platform. A man and two women went over and helped him to get up, . . . but then he fell down again—right on to the tracks!

Page 122, Main Ideas 1

ANNOUNCER: What does the word "hero" mean to you? Maybe you think of superheroes or famous people who do great things. But what about every day ordinary people who help others? Are they heroes too? We begin tonight's program in New York where Brad Peck has the story of the ordinary man that many people are now calling a hero.

REPORTER: It was a Tuesday afternoon at about 12:45, and subway riders were waiting on the platform for their train to arrive.

WOMAN 1: I was standing there waiting for my train, when suddenly, a young man fell down on the platform. A man and two women went over and helped him to get up, . . . but then he fell down again—right on to the tracks!

REPORTER: The young man who fell on to the tracks that day was 20-year-old college student, Cameron Hollopeter.

WOMAN 1: So, this guy was just lying there on the tracks, and he couldn't get up. And then I saw that a train was coming! . . . and then this man, I couldn't believe it, he just jumped down, right into the tracks!

REPORTER: The man who jumped onto the tracks was Wesley Autrey, a 50-year-old construction worker, who was waiting for a train with his two young daughters, ages 4 and 6. When he saw Mr. Hollopeter fall, he reacted immediately. He left his daughters with a woman on the platform, then jumped into the subway tracks to help Mr. Hollopeter.

WOMAN 1: So, at first, he tried to get the young guy back on to the platform. But he couldn't do it. So, he pushed him into the small space between the tracks . . . and he lay down on top of him and held him down to keep him under the train. The train was coming fast into the station, and I . . . I just covered my eyes and waited. I thought they were both gonna die!

REPORTER: The subway train arrived just six seconds after Wesley Autrey jumped down on the tracks. Five cars passed over the top of the two men, less than two inches above Mr. Autrey's head, before it came to a stop.

WOMAN 1: It all happened so fast. I was afraid to open my eyes, but then I heard the man's voice from under the train, calling out "We're OK!" They we both OK! It was amazing—the train passed right over both of 'em!

REPORTER: By acting quickly and holding the man down under the train, Wesley Autrey saved Cameron Hollopeter's life. Richard, another subway rider who saw what happened, praised Mr. Autry's actions.

MAN: It was such a brave thing to do. I was just standing there on the platform, I couldn't move. It took a lot of courage for him to jump onto the train tracks like that. That guy should definitely get a reward for what he did.

REPORTER: Another subway rider, Emily, was concerned about the risk Mr. Autrey took by leaving his two young daughters behind when he jumped on to the tracks.

Audioscript   207

WOMAN 2: I thought about those two young girls . . . they saw their daddy jump onto the tracks. I thought—would they lose their daddy right then and there? Oh my gosh . . . I'm just glad it turned out all right.

REPORTER: Later, when Mr. Autrey was asked why he did it, he said he just saw someone who needed help, and he did what he felt was right. He also thanked his mother, saying that she raised him to believe we should help people whenever we can. He didn't worry about getting hurt; he just thought about saving Cameron Hollopeter from that train.

ANNOUNCER: So, it seems Wesley Autrey doesn't see himself as a hero—just an ordinary guy who did the right thing. That may be true, but people in this community are now calling Wesley Autrey "the Subway Hero."

Page 124, Make Inferences

Excerpt One

WOMAN 1: The train was coming fast into the station, and I . . . I just covered my eyes and waited. I thought they were both gonna die!

Excerpt Two

WOMAN 1: It all happened so fast. I was afraid to open my eyes, but then I heard the man's voice from under the train, calling out "We're OK!" They we both OK! It was amazing—the train passed right over both of 'em!

Excerpt Three

WOMAN 2: I thought about those two young girls . . . they saw their daddy jump onto the tracks. I thought—would they lose their daddy right then and there? Oh my gosh . . . I'm just glad it turned out all right.

Listening Two, page 126, Comprehension

Today, I'd like to talk about altruism. Altruism simply means "showing an unselfish concern for others." In other words, altruism means caring for and helping others without thinking about ourselves. So, altruism can mean doing something brave, such as saving someone from a fire. . . . or it can mean doing something simple, like holding the door open for a stranger, or giving a homeless person some money to buy food. The important point is that you're showing concern for others. Does that make sense?

The problem is that many people don't volunteer to help others—especially in dangerous situations.

In fact, most people just do nothing. Research shows that only about 20 percent of people will take

risks to help others. We also know that some people are more likely to help others in their everyday lives.

But, why is that? Why do some people help out and others don't? Well we don't know for sure, but there's research that shows several possible factors:

One possible factor is the situation we are in. For example, we are much more likely to help someone we know, like friend or family member . . . than a stranger. We are also more likely to help when we are alone compared to when we are in a crowd. For example, if an accident happens, most people usually watch and wait for other people to help out first, but if no one else is there, they are more likely to do something.

Another possible factor is our genes. One study in Germany found that people who have a certain gene are more likely to help others, for example by giving money to those in need. So, maybe some people're just born to help others.

A third possible factor is our personality—the kind of person we are. For example, research shows that people who have positive attitudes, people who expect good things to happen, are also more likely to help others. This could be because they expect that things will turn out OK.

Finally, it may also be the way we are raised. Some people are raised by their families to help others, to feel responsible for others and to show concern for them.

OK, so those are some of the factors that explain altruistic behavior. So, now, let's look at some different kinds of altruism . . .

Page 127, Listening Skill

Excerpt One

PROFESSOR: One possible factor is the situation we are in.

Excerpt Two

PROFESSOR: Another possible factor is our genes.

Excerpt Three

PROFESSOR: Finally, it may also be the way we are raised.

Excerpt Four

PROFESSOR: So, now, let's look at some different kinds of altruism . . .

UNIT 7: Gaming Your Way to Better Health

Listening One, page 146, Preview

ADMINISTRATOR: Good afternoon and thanks for coming. The purpose of today's meeting is to talk about some exciting new technology that the hospital might buy. This technology should help both you—the doctors—and your patients. What I'm talking about is video games. I know, I know, you're probably asking yourselves, what's the connection between video games and healthcare?

Page 146, Main Ideas

ADMINISTRATOR: Good afternoon and thanks for coming. The purpose of today's meeting is to talk about some exciting new technology that the hospital might buy. This technology should help both you—the doctors—and your patients. What I'm talking about is video games. I know, I know, you're probably asking yourselves, what's the connection between video games and healthcare?

Well, the key word is motivation. Now I'm sure none of you has trouble getting your patients to follow all of your instructions, right? I mean, your patients always do everything you tell them to do, no problems, am I right?

So, back to video games and their connection to healthcare. I know that people criticize video games—and that we don't usually hear the words "video game" and "good health" together in one sentence. In fact, just the opposite, right? How about you? When you think of video games, what's the first word that you think of?

AUDIENCE Member 1: Childhood obesity!

AUDIENCE Member 2: Couch potato!

ADMINISTRATOR: Exactly—and I used to think that too. When we hear the words "video game," we often imagine someone who spends all day inside in front of a computer or television screen, who never goes outside, doesn't get any physical exercise—and is overweight or obese as a result. And in fact we all know there is a big problem with that in today's world.

But today I'd like to look at this in a different way—by asking a very simple question, with a simple answer. Why do young people spend so much time playing video games? Because it's fun! And when something is fun, you are motivated to do it. Video games can help you motivate your patients to make the right choices, to follow your instructions, and to stay healthy. It's really that simple. Yes, Sam? You have a question?

DR. SAM: Hmmm . . . I don't know about this. I mean, I know it's sometimes hard to get patients to do what's best for their health, but I'm not sure games are the answer. Isn't that just putting a Band-Aid on a much deeper problem? I think we need to motivate our patients to *want* to take care of their health, to realize that it's really for their own good.

ADMINISTRATOR: I understand your concerns, Sam, I really do, but maybe if I give you a specific example you'll have a better idea of what I'm talking about.

DR. SAM: Ok, go ahead. I'm all ears.

ADMINISTRATOR: Well, one game I'm really excited about is for kids with diabetes. You know how hard it is to get kids to test their blood sugar? Well, this game makes it fun. The test is a part of the game—in the game, the kid with diabetes is a superhero whose powers get stronger every time he checks his blood sugar. So he gets a reward for doing something that kids with diabetes usually hate doing. That's just one example of how you use a game to motivate kids to follow your instructions—and to be healthy.

DR. JOE: Actually, I think that sounds like a great idea. I see a lot of kids with diabetes, and it's so hard to get them to do what they need to do to stay healthy. After all, their lives aren't easy—what kid wants to watch what they eat . . . and prick themselves with a needle? I'm all for anything that can make these poor kids' lives more fun.

DR. BRENDA: Well, I can see how this might work with kids, but most of us work with adults.

ADMINISTRATOR: I'm glad you said that, Brenda. In fact, the games we're looking at are not just for kids. Let me give you another example of an amazing game that works well for both kids and adults. It's called Snow World. It was created to help patients with very bad burns. Patients play the game while doctors and nurses are cleaning their burns—something that, as you all know, is very, very painful. The patients put on special glasses and earplugs and get lost in the game. A number of studies show that patients playing Snow World during burn treatment have a lot less pain.

ADMINISTRATOR: Anyway, I know you all have patients to see, so I'll let you go. But you'll get an email later today with a link to some of the games we're looking at. When you get a minute, take a look.

Page 149, Make Inferences

Excerpt One

ADMINISTRATOR: Exactly—and I used to think that too. When we hear the words "video game," we often imagine someone who spends all day inside in front of a computer or television screen, who never goes outside, doesn't get any physical exercise—and is overweight or obese as a result. And in fact we all know there is a big problem with that in today's world.

But today I'd like to look at this in a different way—by asking a very simple question, with a simple answer. Why do young people spend so much time playing video games? Because it's fun!

Excerpt Two

ADMINISTRATOR: I understand your concerns, Sam, I really do, but maybe if I give you a specific example you'll have a better idea of what I'm talking about.

Listening Two, page 151, Comprehension

MALE PROFESSOR (MP): So, how are things going with the latest group of students?

FEMALE PROFESSOR (FP): Great! I have a pretty talented group this year. And they just love the new video games and simulations. I can't believe their enthusiasm.

MP: Yeah, well mine are spending a lot of time in the simulation lab too—but I'm not sure how much they're really learning. Seems to me that the time they're spending on games is time they aren't spending doing the class readings.

FP: Really? Not my students. Actually, just the opposite. This group's doing a really good job with the readings, compared to last year. Do you use a reward system—you know, like making them pass an online quiz on the reading before they can use the simulation lab? That works pretty well for me.

MP: No, I didn't think of that—maybe I'll try it.

FP: I'd be happy to share my quizzes with you.

MP: Thanks. I appreciate it. But back to the simulation lab . . . do you really think that it's helping them improve their skills? Personally, I'm not convinced that working on a dummy is the same as working on a living, breathing human being.

FP: Well . . . actually I wasn't sure at first either, but after using the simulation lab for a couple of semesters, I'm becoming more and more convinced.

MP: Are you sure? . . . But what about their communication skills? Don't you think you have to interact with a real person to develop those?

FP: No, not really. I was surprised at how well the dummies behave just like real human beings—with one important difference—you can't hurt or kill them! And the research shows they really work.

MP: Which research?

FP: Well, I read some studies that show medical students trained on video games and dummies improve both their skills and general medical knowledge. In fact, they say using games works better than more traditional training—you know, like the way we were trained. Because of all the practice with the dummies, they make fewer mistakes on the real patients. At least that's been my experience—and the research supports it.

MP: Hmmm . . . , I'd like to see the research you're talking about. Could you send me a link?

FP: Sure, no problem.

MP: Oh, and a link to those quizzes, too.

FP: Absolutely. Anyway, I have to run, but I'm glad we had the chance to chat.

MP: Me too—always great talking to you, and thanks for the ideas and information.

FP: Any time. Good luck with the quizzes—let me know if they work for you.

MP: Sure, see you around.

FP: See you later.

Page 152, Listening Skill

Excerpt One

DR. JOE: . . . I'm all for anything that can make these poor kids' lives more fun.

DR. BRENDA: Well, I can see how this might work with kids, but most of us work with adults.

Excerpt Two

FP: Well . . . actually I wasn't sure at first either, but after using the simulation lab for a couple of semesters, I'm becoming more and more convinced.

MP: Are you sure? . . . But what about their communication skills? Don't you think you have to interact with a real person to develop those?

UNIT 8: Endangered Languages

Listening One, page 170, Preview

PROFESSOR: Good morning, everybody. Today, I'd like to talk about endangered and dead languages. So . . . who did the reading for today? Hm . . . I see . . . *some* of you did. . . . Then, who can tell me what a dead language is?

STUDENT 1: Um . . . Is it a language that nobody speaks anymore, you know, like Latin?

PROFESSOR: Yeah, that's right. Now, how about an endangered language? Jessica, what do you think?

STUDENT 2: An endangered language? Well, uh . . . maybe it's a language that might die?

PROFESSOR: Right. An endangered language is a language that may die, or become extinct soon. There are over 6,000 languages in the world, and some linguists think that about 50 percent could be extinct by the year 2100. Yes, that's a lot! So, many linguists want to preserve these dying languages.

Page 170, Main Ideas

PROFESSOR: Good morning, everybody. Today, I'd like to talk about endangered and dead languages. So . . . who did the reading for today? Hm . . . I see . . . *some* of you did. . . . Then, who can tell me what a dead language is?

Student 1: Um . . . Is it a language that nobody speaks anymore, you know, like Latin?

Professor: Yeah, that's right. Now, how about an endangered language? Jessica, what do you think?

Student 2: An endangered language? Well, uh . . . maybe it's a language that might die?

Professor: Right. An endangered language is a language that may die, or become extinct soon. There are over 6,000 languages in the world, and some linguists think that about 50 percent could be extinct by the year 2100. Yes, that's a lot! So, many linguists want to preserve these dying languages.

Student 2: So, why do they want to do *that*? There are so many languages! Isn't it easier when people speak the same language anyway?

Professor: Well, that's a good point. Having fewer languages is more convenient for communication, but there are good reasons to save endangered languages. When a language dies, part of the culture can die, too. Now this doesn't *always* happen. For instance, the Manx people on the Isle of Man in the Irish Sea lost their native language, but they've kept many parts of their culture and traditions as Manx. But when a language dies it usually has a big affect on the culture. Think about what is expressed through language: stories, ceremonies, poetry, humor, a whole way of thinking and feeling. When a language dies, all of this may be lost. So, culture is lost. Also, history and knowledge are passed down through language, so when the language disappears, important history and knowledge may be lost, too. So that's why people care about language loss. All right . . . moving on . . . Now, how do you think languages become endangered and extinct?

Student 3: Well, I guess nobody speaks them or studies them.

Professor: Yes. And there are several reasons why languages can become endangered. One reason is sometimes the government makes it illegal to teach the language in school. For example, before 1987, it was illegal to teach the Hawaiian language in Hawaii's public schools. It was difficult for children to acquire Hawaiian. As a result, that language became endangered. But, starting in 1987, new programs began to teach the Hawaiian language. Today, there are more than 2,000 students enrolled in these programs. So now, many children have the chance to learn Hawaiian and preserve it for the future.

In another situation, if one community has more power than another community, the less powerful community often feels it must learn the language of the more powerful or dominant group. Two things can happen in this situation. In one case, the more dominant language replaces the other language. One example is the case of Native American languages spoken in what is now the United States. Once, there were hundreds of Native American languages. Now, more and more people speak English, and not the native languages. Many of these languages have become extinct.

So, sometimes a community totally replaces their native language with another language. Or, the less powerful community can keep their native language and learn the other language, too. An example of this is in Greenland where students learn Kalaallisut and Danish. They are bilingual; they learn both languages, so they won't lose their native language. Also, Kalaallisut was made an official language in Greenland, along with Danish. This can also help save endangered languages for future generations.

Student 3: So . . . Are people doing anything else to save the dying languages?

Professor: Yes, linguists help create community programs where people can study the language and learn about the culture. Also, they try to preserve as many endangered languages as they can. They make videotapes, audiotapes, and written records of language with translations. They also study the vocabulary and rules of the language, and write dictionaries and grammar books.

OK, that's a lot of information for one lecture! We talked about endangered and dying languages and why it's important to save languages, how languages die, and how people can save endangered languages. Great! So for next time, please read chapter ten.

Page 172, Make Inferences

Excerpt One

Professor: Yes. And there are several reasons why languages can become endangered. One reason is sometimes the government makes it illegal to teach the language in school. For example, before 1987, it was illegal to teach the Hawaiian language in Hawaii's public schools. It was difficult for children to acquire Hawaiian. As a result, that language became endangered. But, starting in 1987, new programs began to teach the Hawaiian language. Today, there are more than 2,000 students enrolled in these programs. So now, many children have the chance to learn Hawaiian and preserve it for the future.

Excerpt Two

Professor: So, many linguists want to preserve these dying languages.

STUDENT 2: So, why do they want to do *that*? There are so many languages! Isn't it easier when people speak the same language anyway?

Listening Two, page 175, Comprehension

WOMAN: I am Maori, living in New Zealand. In school, I learned and spoke English. This is because English was the official language. Everything was taught in English in school. That was the government policy. I only heard Maori when I was with my grandparents. I could understand a little Maori, but could not speak it. I could not have a conversation with my grandparents because they did not speak English.

When I was in school, I knew that I was not learning the Maori culture. As a result, I felt separated from my grandparents. I felt empty inside and different from my family.

Maori is an endangered language and if children stop learning it, it will eventually die. I do not want to see Maori disappear. So now that I am an adult and have children of my own, I decided I wanted my children to learn their native language. I found a preschool that teaches children Maori before they enter school where they will learn English. The schools are called "language nests." Language nests began in 1981, when a group of Maori leaders saw that Maori was endangered and dying. They decided to do something. They did not want to wait for the government to do anything, so they got together and came up with the idea of preschools where children can learn Maori. Now, there are over 400 language nests and more than 9,000 children go to school at language nests. Language nests are a big part of Maori education.

Through the language nests, children learn about the values and traditions of the Maori culture. For example, we have a strong belief in love, compassion, caring, hospitality, family responsibilities, and respect for elders. Also, children learn our Maori stories, which are a big part of our tradition. So, children learn about Maori culture, as well as the language.

We are also trying to help adults learn Maori. For instance, I now attend classes that meet in a neighborhood center, where the teachers are all older Maoris, usually grandparents. Another way adults can learn is by attending week-long classes. In these courses, no English is spoken all week! Everything is Maori. Now there are many more adults who speak Maori, and this encourages our children who are also learning Maori. Language classes have really helped to preserve Maori.

Also, in 1987, the government recognized Maori as the official language of New Zealand, with English, too. This will also help preserve the Maori language.

Page 177, Listening Skill

Excerpt One

WOMAN: We are also trying to help adults learn Maori. For instance, I now attend classes that meet in a neighborhood center, where the teachers are all older Maoris, usually grandparents. Another way adults can learn is by attending week-long classes. In these courses, no English is spoken all week! Everything is Maori.

Excerpt Two

PROFESSOR: Now, how do you think languages become endangered and extinct?

STUDENT 3: Well, I guess nobody speaks them or studies them.

PROFESSOR: Yes. And there are several reasons why languages can become endangered. One reason is sometimes the government makes it illegal to teach the language in school. For example, before 1987, it was illegal to teach the Hawaiian language in Hawaii's public schools. It was difficult for children to acquire Hawaiian.

Page 178, Connect the Listenings, Step One: Organize

Excerpt One

WOMAN: In school, I learned and spoke English. This is because English was the official language. Everything was taught in English in school. That was the government policy.

Excerpt Two

WOMAN: I only heard Maori when I was with my grandparents. I could understand a little Maori, but could not speak it. I could not have a conversation with my grandparents because they did not speak English.

Excerpt Three

WOMAN: When I was in school, I knew that I was not learning the Maori culture. As a result, I felt separated from my grandparents. I felt empty inside and different from my family.

Excerpt Four

WOMAN: I found a preschool that teaches children Maori before they enter school where they will learn English. The schools are called "language nests." Language nests began in 1981, when a group of Maori leaders saw that Maori was endangered and dying. They decided to do something. They did not want to wait for the government to do anything, so they got together and came up with the idea of preschools where children could learn Maori. Now, there are over 400 language nests and more than 9,000 children go to school at language nests. Language nests are a big part of Maori education.

Excerpt Five

WOMAN: Also, in 1987, the government recognized Maori as the official language of New Zealand, with English, too. This will also help preserve the Maori language.

Excerpt Six

WOMAN: We are also trying to help adults learn Maori. For instance, I now attend classes that meet in a neighborhood center, where the teachers are all older Maoris, usually grandparents. Another way adults can learn is by attending week-long classes. In these courses, no English is spoken all week!

THE PHONETIC ALPHABET

Consonant Symbols

/b/	be	/t/	to
/d/	do	/v/	van
/f/	father	/w/	will
/g/	get	/y/	yes
/h/	he	/z/	zoo, busy
/k/	keep, can	/θ/	thanks
/l/	let	/ð/	then
/m/	may	/ʃ/	she
/n/	no	/ʒ/	vision, Asia
/p/	pen	/tʃ/	child
/r/	rain	/dʒ/	join
/s/	so, circle	/ŋ/	long

Vowel Symbols

/ɑ/	far, hot	/iy/	we, mean, feet
/ɛ/	met, said	/ey/	day, late, rain
/ɔ/	tall, bought	/ow/	go, low, coat
/ə/	son, under	/uw/	too, blue
/æ/	cat	/ay/	time, buy
/ɪ/	ship	/aw/	house, now
/ʊ/	good, could, put	/oy/	boy, coin